O9-BTI-803

A Key
To The
Parables

A KEY
TO THE
PARABLES

(An Original Deus Book)

by Wilfrid J. Harrington, O.P.

PAULIST PRESS DEUS BOOKS

NEW YORK   GLEN ROCK   WESTMINSTER
TORONTO   AMSTERDAM

NIHIL OBSTAT: Fr. Augustinus Flannery, O.P., S.T.D.
Fr. Hieronymus Murphy-O'Connor, O.P., S.T.D., B.S.S.

IMPRIMI POTEST: Fr. Ludovicus C. Coffey, O.P.
Prov. Hib. Prior Provincialis.
die 20 Septembris 1963.

NIHIL OBSTAT: John A. Goodwine, J.C.D.
Censor Librorum

IMPRIMATUR: ✠ Francis Cardinal Spellman
Archbishop of New York

June 11, 1964

The Nihil Obstat and Imprimatur are official declarations that a book or pamphlet is free of doctrinal or moral error. No implication is contained therein that those who have granted the Nihil Obstat and Imprimatur agree with the contents, opinions or statements expressed.

COVER DESIGN: Claude Ponsot

Copyright © 1964 by
The Missionary Society
of St. Paul the Apostle
in the State of New York

Library of Congress
Catalog Card Number: 64-24516

Published by the Paulist Press
Editorial Office: 304 W. 58th St., N.Y., N.Y. 10019
Business Office: Glen Rock, New Jersey 07452

Manufactured in the
United States of America
by Our Sunday Visitor Press

Contents

Acknowledgments

Almost all the material of Part I has appeared in *Doctrine and Life,* Feb. - May 1963. I owe a special debt of gratitude to the Editor, Rev. Austin Flannery, O.P., not just for permission to reproduce the articles in question but, rather, for having commissioned them in the first place and then for encouraging me to develop them into a book.

New Testament quotations in Part II are taken from *The New Testament of Our Lord and Saviour Jesus Christ,* translated into English from the original Greek by Francis Aloysius Spencer, O.P., edited by Charles J. Callan, O.P. and John A. McHugh, O.P. Copyright 1937 by The Macmillan Company and used with permission.

Preface

Though it is sadly true that too many Catholics still have scarcely more than a passing acquaintance with the New Testament, all have some familiarity with the parables. We have learned a little about them at school, and year after year we listen to certain of them at Mass. Now, familiarity may be deceptive—it can give the illusion that one has grasped something merely because it has been heard repeatedly. All too often, in fact, we start off with a restricted, or with a mistaken view, and never get any further. Most of us, for instance, are surely unaware that the parables, as they stand in the gospels, may not have quite the meaning they had when first spoken by our Lord. But if it is true that there has been a change of meaning then, obviously, it is imperative, in each case, to discover the change and the reason for it. And if we cannot, to some extent at least, establish the original sense of a parable, it is obvious that we are going to miss something of it.

The purpose of these pages is to show how we may replace the parables in their first setting, the ministry of Jesus. PART I will be concerned largely with the reasons that led the first Christians to reinterpret and adapt the parables and with an examination of their techniques and methods. If we can discern the motives that moved them we may ultimately understand the original thrust of a parable. PART II, a study of the parables of the third gospel, will illustrate the tendency I speak of and will, I hope, demonstrate the positive advantages of this approach.

A select bibliography lists the authors on whom I have leaned almost exclusively; this acknowledgment will stand in place of references that would soon become tiresome. However, I cannot, in this casual way, pass over my particularly heavy indebtedness to the classic work of Joachim Jeremias. Though I have not always accepted his views, there is hardly a page that does not owe something to him.

The reader may well wonder why, in PART II, I have confined myself to St. Luke. The reason is simple and prosaic: if I had not taken this somewhat ruthless step the book might never have been finished. And even if the third gospel does contain most of the recorded parables of our Lord, it is, nevertheless, a disadvantage that the scope had not been wider. I can only hope that the study will be of some help to those who are anxious to have a better understanding of the parables.

W. J. H.

PART I
APPROACH
TO THE
PARABLES

1
He Spoke to Them
in Parables

When modern scholars start studying the first three gospels, they are inclined to give precedence to Mark. It is the earliest of the gospels as they have come down to us and so is considered to be, on the whole, closest to the beginning of the gospel tradition. Though the position is not quite as simple as all that, this attitude is justified. But it is a recent development and it was Matthew and not Mark that quickly became the most widely known and read of the gospels. The reason is not hard to find. It is simply that St. Matthew has many more sayings of our Lord than St. Mark and, unlike St. Luke, he has arranged them neatly in five great discourses. Accordingly, when Christians wished to study the teaching of Christ they turned instinctively to Matthew; there they found the very words of Christ.

The Words of Christ

The "very words of Christ"? Today we are hardly so sanguine. We not only see the relative importance of the gospels in a new light, but we also take a more realistic view of the formation of the gospels; and we have also learned to analyze the gospel material. With regard to the sayings of our Lord we do find that the same sayings are recorded mainly by the first three evangelists, though St. Mark has fewer of these than the others. And rarely do we find that any saying occurs, in identical form, in any two gospels. Generally, the differences are insignificant but frequently enough they are more far-reaching. However, we must view the problem in proper perspective.

It would be unreasonable to expect that the words of our Lord always would be recorded in just the same way. Indeed it is impossible to have any of his sayings *exactly* as they came from his lips, for the very good reason that he spoke Aramaic and our gospels were written in Greek. What we do have is a translation of sayings of our Lord, and a translation does not have to be slavishly literal. A saying or passage can be rendered quite faithfully in more than one form by the use of synonyms, and stylistic changes will not alter the sense.

While this may explain many of the variations that we discern in the sayings of Christ, there are explanations that go much deeper. We have to look to the beginning, to the apostolic Church which gave the gospel story its shape. The first problem that confronted the apostles when they set about their task of preaching Christ was how to present that message and, for practical missionary purposes, a selection had to be made from his words as well as from his works. Very often sayings were preserved because they solved some pressing problem or pointed the way to a particular line of conduct.

There was also, and for the same reason, a certain amount of adaptation and interpretation; the Church lived by the teaching of Christ—its role was not limited to a mechanical passing on of his words. Then came the evangelist with his contribution. His work was not a private undertaking, he was, in fact, the last link in a chain. The gospel, founded on the works and words of Christ, was first lived in the Church, and the evangelist, though directly inspired by God, was also the spokesman of a Church guided by the Spirit of God. Yet, the evangelists are authors, and the gospels are personal works, each having its own definite stamp and character. So the evangelist, too, further interpreted and adapted the teaching of the living Lord.

All this is undeniable, however we may feel that there is still one special kind of teaching in which we can hope to catch the actual accents of Christ. Surely the parables still speak his language? A modern scholar, in the opening sentence of a masterly study of the parables,[1] anticipates this question: "The student of the parables of Jesus, as they have been transmitted to us in the first three gospels, stands upon particularly firm historical ground; they are a fragment of the original rock of the tradition." Here, then, more easily than elsewhere, we can indeed hope not only to discern the authentic teaching of our Lord (that is everywhere in the gospels) but to hear that teaching in his own words.

Therefore, should we merely read the parables as they stand? No, because it is not as simple as that. As we shall see the parables, too, have been adapted by the Church and the evangelists. Now this is not only understandable, it was inevitable. The circumstances of the early Church were not those of the ministry of Jesus, and if the parables were to suit later needs they had to be adapted to some extent. Thus, the parables have two settings—their original setting in the ministry of Christ and their later setting in the life of the primitive Church, and it is only by giving full weight to the Church's role in the formation of the gospels that we can arrive at the original setting of the parables. This, we believe, will be evident when we come to study the process in some individual parables.

Parable and Allegory

Perhaps next we should determine what is meant by "parable". "At its simplest the parable is a simile drawn from nature or common life, arresting the hearer by its vividness or strangeness, and leaving the mind in sufficient doubt to tease it into active thought."[2] But the simile may be developed into a story and, indeed, this is what we commonly understand a parable to be.

A distinctive feature is that the typical parable, whether it be long or short, presents one single point of comparison; the details have no independent significance. This last distinguishes the parable from the allegory, for in an allegory each detail has a symbolic significance. Thus, in

Paul's allegory of *The Olive Tree* (Rom. 11, 16-24) the olive tree is the people of God, the branches of the wild olive are Gentile Christians and the branches that have been cut off are the unbelieving Jews. The symbolical value of the details is deliberately contrived by Paul and they are meant to be interpreted in that sense. It would, however, be absurd to apply the same canon to a parable as, for instance, to find some special significance in the *dramatis personae* of *The Good Samaritan,* and even in the two cents given to the innkeeper. The details are there simply to build up the story.

It was necessary to distinguish between parable and allegory, but the distinction must not be pressed too rigorously. It is not at all uncommon, especially in an extended parable, that certain details may be inserted precisely because they suit the intended application. Even more important is the fact that the word *parabole* (parable), as it occurs in the New Testament, has a wide range. It comes from the Greek translation of the Old Testament where it renders the Hebrew *mashal,* a term that includes figurative forms of speech of every kind—not only simple sayings but even riddles and fables as well as parable and allegory. Thus in a biblical context *parabole* is not the parable in its narrow sense—a form of Greek rhetoric. Even apart from the Old Testament background it is common sense that a Greek criterion may not be applied, without more ado, to the utterly Semitic character of the parables of Jesus.

In fact, we find that the gospel parables—in

the wider connotation just indicated—are not to be grouped together in one neat category. They range from figurative sayings ("Beware of the leaven of the Pharisees"; "if the blind lead the blind, both fall into the ditch"), through similitudes or pictures, (*e.g.* The Fig Tree as Herald of Summer), to the parable proper, which is a story.

The difference between a similitude and a parable is that the similitude is concerned with some general truth or process (like the seasonal significance of a leafing tree or the action of leaven) whereas the parable describes what one man—or class of men—did ("a sower went out to sow"; the action of the laborers in the vineyard). It is not possible to draw a precise line between the three classes of parables since one class overlaps another. Nevertheless, we may apply a rough grammatical test and say that the figurative saying has no more than one verb, the similitude more than one verb and the parable a series of verbs in the past tense.[3]

The Gospel Parables

Despite the variety of form, all of the gospel parables are true to nature and to life. Each similitude or story gives an authentic picture of things that actually happen. Of course, we must remember that the background of these parables is always Palestinian. It is important to have this in mind when we interpret the parables. To our eyes the farmer of *The Sower* is singularly careless as he scatters his seed heedlessly in all directions. We judge his methods very differently when we realize that in Palestine sowing precedes plowing and hence, in the parable, the sower is depicted as striding over the unplowed stubble field. Now we understand why he "sows on the path": he sows intentionally on the path that the villagers have made by treading over the stubble because the path is going to be plowed up (and the seed plowed in at the same time). He sows intentionally among the withered thorns because these, too, are going to be plowed up. He just cannot avoid the rocks because much of Palestine's terrain is more harsh than Kansas.

What appears to westerners as sheer incompetence is normal procedure under Palestinian conditions. Or if it happens that the actions of persons in the parables are surprising, the point is that such actions *are* surprising. The conduct of the employer who pays the same wages for one hour's work as for twelve is quite unusual, but the surprise of the laborers at being treated so gives point to the story. When we give full weight to this aspect of the parables (the local color), we must realize that we are right back at the beginning of the the gospel tradition and stand very close to Jesus himself.

We may still wonder, of course, why our Lord used parables at all or, at least, why he used them so widely. The reason is very simple: he wanted to teach people and parables are teaching media. Besides, here was a method that was familiar to his audience, for the rabbis, even early in the 1st century A.D., made frequent use of the parable. This is not at all surprising since it is a method that had a particular appeal for Semites; the parable is colorful and concrete, quite unlike the abstract reasoning of the Greeks.

Apart from the fact that the rabbis had, in a sense, prepared the way, these rabbinical parables can also help our understanding of the parables of Jesus. We find, for instance, that many of his parables have introductory formulas, the most common one being: "The kingdom of God is like a sower", and so on. Now the point is that the kingdom of God is *not* like a sower, and the current rendering of the phrase can be misleading. The rabbis usually began their parables with the words: "A parable: it is like . . ." which was a conventional abbreviation of: "I will tell you a parable. With what may the matter be compared? It is the case with it as with . . ." We find evidence of a similar formula in the gospels. Thus Mark 4, 30f: "With what can we compare the kingdom of God or by what parable shall we describe it? It is like . . ."; and Luke 13, 20f: "To what shall I compare the kingdom of God? It is like . . ."

In view of this we should recognize that wherever "is like" occurs in the introduction of a parable it stands for the whole formula: "It is the case with . . . as with . . ." This is not pedantry but has an immediate bearing on the correct interpretation of the parables. So, in Matthew 13, 31 we should realize that the introductory formula: "The kingdom of heaven is like a grain of mustard seed" really means: "It is the case with the kingdom of heaven as with a grain of mustard seed", that is to say, the kingdom of God is not compared to the grain of seed but to the tall shrub that grows out of the seed. Similarly, in Matthew 13, 33 the kingdom of heaven is not like leaven but like the prepared, risen dough. And in quite the same way, the kingdom in Matthew 13, 45 is not "like a merchant" but like a pearl; in Matthew 25, 1 it is not "like ten virgins" but like a wedding; in Matthew 22, 2 it is not "like a king" but like a wedding-feast; in Matthew 13, 24 it is not "like a man who sowed good seed" but like the harvest.

In his parables Jesus put before his listeners the homely sights and activities of the country and country life to such an extent that it would be obvious from this alone that he was country-bred. He drew lessons from the lives of men and women like themselves, real men and women, and the language of these stories was their own everyday speech. But the message was not always crystal clear and the parables were designed to make them think; after all this is a feature of true pedagogy and we should expect no less from the supreme teacher.

A parable catches the imagination and wins ready attention but its ultimate appeal is to the intelligence. It is by no means just a simple illustration addressed to unlettered folk incapable of serious thought but is primarily meant to stir up spiritual perception. It is significant that (as we shall see) Jesus addressed a high proportion of his parables to the Jewish intelligentsia. The whole scope of the technique is put neatly for us by St. Mark: "With many such parables he spoke the word to them, *as they were able to hear it*" (4, 33).

The Purpose of the Parables

Yet earlier the same St. Mark has stated a motive for the use of parables that appears to be a flat contradiction of the view just indicated. Indeed, it is a motive that seems to strike at the very purpose of the parable and makes nonsense of all that we have written until now. The text that has caused so much difficulty reads:

> And when he was alone, those who were about him with the Twelve asked him concerning the parables. And he said to them: To you has been given the secret of the kingdom of God, but for those outside everything is in parables; "so that they may indeed see but not perceive, and may indeed hear but not understand, lest they should turn again and be forgiven" (Mark 4, 10-12).[4]

To some this has seemed to mean that our Lord used parables as a deliberate veiling of the truth: the unbelieving multitudes were punished for their lack of faith. It is pretty obvious that such a theory would never have been aired except for that troublesome text of St. Mark. But to base an interpretation on this one passage, which upsets the notion of parable and which demands of our Lord a thoroughly uncharacteristic attitude, is surely an extreme example of the tail wagging the dog. No one today would defend a similar position or question the soundness of the following judgment: "That Jesus desired not to be understood by the people in general, and therefore clothed his teaching in unintelligible forms, cannot be made credible on any reasonable reading of the gospels."[5]

If such is the case we must see whether the text of Mark cannot be interpreted in a manner consonant with the whole spirit of the gospel.[6] The very first thing we must recognize is that Mark 4, 11-12 is a saying that has no real link with its context (verse 13 logically follows verse 10). It has been added here, either by St. Mark or by his source, because of the word "parables" that occurs in it. This technique of joining together different sayings of our Lord by means of catchwords is not unusual in the gospels; we have, for example, a whole series of sayings linked together in this way in Mark 9, 33-50.

Next we have to recall the very wide range of the Hebrew word *mashal* from which "parable" is derived in the gospels. Then we find in verse 11 a contrast between the disciples ("to you") and the others ("those outside") and, according to the rules of the Semitic construction called parallelism — which apply in this verse — the same contrast should exist between "secret" (literally "mystery") and "parable", this parallel does exist when *parabole* is given the more literal meaning of its Hebrew equivalent: "riddle", "a dark saying." We now have the required antithesis: to you the secret is revealed—those outside are confronted by riddles; and we may render the second half of verse 11: "But for those outside all things are obscure."

Verse 12 is a (rather free) quotation of Isa. 6, 9f. This grim declaration must be understood in its Hebrew idiom and with a realization of the customary Old Testament neglect of secondary causes. It is not God who blinds men to the truth; that blindness is their own fault. What the text really means is that God clearly foresees that the people will not listen to his prophet. A study of the gospels must surely convince us that the passage can be fittingly applied to our Lord and his teaching.[7] The phrase "in order that" which introduces the quotation is a conventional abbreviation, and the full introductory formula would read: "In order that the Scripture might be fulfilled, which says . . ."

In the light of this rather tedious explanation —one which was required because of the misunderstanding that has often clouded the text— we may render the passage:

> To you has God[8] given the secret of the kingdom of God, but for those outside everything is obscure; in order that (as it is written) "they may indeed see but not perceive, and may indeed hear and yet not understand, unless they turn and God will forgive them."

The saying deals not with parables but with the Lord's teaching in general. It concerns the "secret of the kingdom" which is revealed to the disciples and not to all. What is this secret? It is the fact that the kingdom is already present in the person of Jesus and in his works. By dint of patient teaching the disciples had arrived at a realization of this truth (a realization that was very imperfect until the great light of the Resurrection had shone upon it), but the people had quite failed to recognize the signs of the times (Luke 12, 54-59). It is, no doubt, in view of the Jewish rejection of Christ—the terrible blindness of Israel of which St. Paul speaks—that the saying was remembered in the early Church. St. Mark is here reflecting that not even the parables had won over the listeners to faith. But the main point is the special formation that the disciples, and they alone, received.

In his parables, as in the Sermon on the Mount and in all his teaching, Jesus spoke to the people "as they were able to hear", and the force of this is not impaired by St. Mark's further comment: "but privately to his own disciples he explained everything" (4, 34).

That was the way Christ had planned it. His work was to be carried on and completed by his Church, and the disciples whom he instructed and formed were the foundation of that Church. As a vital and growing reality the Church of Christ not only lived by his words but also felt free to adapt those words to fit the changed circumstances after the Resurrection. The parables could not have been an exception.

2

The Interpretation
of the Parables

Even a superficial reading of the gospels will show how widely our Lord employed the parable. And it is not surprising that from the earliest days of the Church the interpretation of these parables should have been a constant preoccupation. The interpretation, on the whole rather constant, manifests especially one consistent tendency to allegorize wherever possible. In the foregoing chapter we have noticed the difference between parable and allegory, but have also admitted that the distinction between them is not always maintained in practice. We shall see that already in the primitive Church—the evidence is in the gospels—there was a move to bestow allegorical significance to the details of what was originally a pure parable and to heighten that significance where it already existed. However, for the moment we shall consider only the interpretation of the parables from the patristic age onward.

Allegorization

Though the great Scripture scholar Origen was not the first to allegorize the parables, he was the first to push the method to its limit, or what must have seemed the limit, because, in due course, later generations were to out-origen Origen. For example this is what he makes of *The Laborers in the Vineyard:* The first batch of workers signifies the generations from the creation to Noah; the second those from Noah to Abraham; the third those from Abraham to Moses; the fourth those from Moses to Josue; the fifth those up to the time of Christ. The householder is God, the penny represents salvation.

He treats *The Good Samaritan* in the following fashion: The man who fell among thieves is Adam. Jerusalem represents heaven and Jericho is the world. The robbers are the devil and his angels. The priest stands for the Law, the Levite for the prophets. The Good Samaritan is Christ himself and the beast on which the wounded man was set is Christ's body which bears the fallen Adam. The inn is the Church; the two pennies the Father and the Son; and the Samaritan's promise to return, Christ's second coming.[1]

And if we imagine that ingenuity could go no further, let us listen to the great Augustine on the same theme. He follows the lines of Origen but adds some refinements of his own: Jericho means the moon and signifies our mortality because it is born, waxes, wanes and dies. The robbers, that is, the devils, stripped Adam of his immortality, beat him by persuading him to sin and left him half-dead, that is, wasted and oppressed by sin.

The binding of the wounds is the curbing of sin; oil is hope and wine is fervor. The seating on the beast is belief in the Incarnation. The inn is the Church, the next day is the time after the Resurrection of Christ and the two pennies are either the two commandments of love, or the promise of this life and of the life to come. The innkeeper is St. Paul.[2]

Most of the Fathers handled the parables in much the same manner and the method has persisted through the Middle Ages and down to our own time. A modern example in a book taken at random from the homiletics shelves of a theological library shows that the process has lost nothing over the centuries.

Once again, *The Good Samaritan:* "The man who fell among the robbers is an image of the human race which, through disobedience, fell from the state of grace into a state of sin. (This is hardly fair to the unfortunate traveler of the parable!) The wound of mankind was mortal but it could be cured. But the cure could be effected only by the Good Samaritan—that is, the Eternal Word, a stranger to us because he is God . . . This Divine Samaritan, in order to heal our wounds, first assumed our nature. He treated our spiritual wounds with the oil of grace and the wine of heavenly charity. He bound up these wounds with the bandages of his holy love, and he brought us to the inn of salvation, to the bosom of Holy Church, where we are under the protection of his ministers whose office it is to heal our infirmities and prepare us for eternal life. To his priests he gave two most efficient means of providing for our wants. These means are: instructions and the sacraments."[3]

Now, of course, the doctrine put forward in these interpretations is good, sound, Christian doctrine—and a sermon prepared along those lines might be effective—but it is decidedly not the teaching of the parable. And, after all, when we study the parables we are not primarily interested in whatever preachers or exegetes, whether these be our own contemporaries or Fathers of the Church, have read into them, but in what our Lord himself intended them to mean. Nor is it any disparagement of the Fathers to recognize that modern scientific exegesis has made decided advances on their technique—the biblical scholarship of centuries has not been barren. In the present case, we must acknowledge that the allegorical method has very often effectively cloaked the original message of the parables. It is one of the aims of this chapter to emphasize the necessity of boldly stripping away the strident superimposed colors in order to win back the quiet beauty of the masterpiece that lies beneath.

But we must be careful not to go to the other extreme and deny that our Lord ever wove allegorical traits into his parables. We must also candidly admit that the gospels themselves give evidence that the tendency was present in the Church from the beginning. And we must honestly acknowledge that, in view of changed circumstances, the tendency was not only legitimate but inevitable. However, it was kept within bounds and there is not a trace in the gospels of the extravagance of later times when ingenuity became the only criterion. Yet even within the gospel itself it is still infinitely worthwhile to place each parable—wherever possible—in the historical background of our Lord's life and to hear it once more from his own lips.

The Great Feast

It is instructive to watch the allegorical method at work in the primitive Church. We may illustrate it by comparing two versions of the same parable, that of *The Great Feast*. In Luke 14, 16-24 it reads as follows:

A man once gave a big dinner party and had invited many. When the time came for the dinner he sent his servant to tell the people he had invited: "Come, everything is now ready." They began one and all to excuse themselves. The first said to him: "I have bought a field and I must go and look at it. Please excuse me." Another one said: "I have bought five yoke of oxen, and I am on my way to try them out. Please excuse me." And another one said: "I have just married and so cannot come." Then the servant went back and told all this to his master. The master of the house was very angry and said to his servant, "Go out quickly into the streets and alleys of the town and bring in here the poor and crippled and blind and lame." "Sir," said the servant, "your orders have been carried out and still there is room." Then the master said to his servant, "Go out to the highways and hedgerows and make them come in, so that my house may be full. For I tell you that not one of those I invited shall taste my dinner."

This is a straightforward parable and must be very close to the original Aramaic form. There is only one detail that would seem to be an allegorical development and that is the double summoning of the ultimate guests. Those within the city are doubtless the publicans and sinners, and so we have the familiar contrast between them and the rejected leaders of the people; the invitation to those outside the city can only refer to the Gentiles. The intention is, perhaps, not altogether clear, but the special interest in the Gentile mission does appear to betray the hand of St. Luke. What is obvious, at any rate, is that the development is unforced and far removed from the fantastic applications we have met with earlier.

The essential point of the parable is very clearly the refusal of the invited guests and their replacement by others. The parable is addressed by Jesus to his critics and opponents, in defense of the gospel and of his own conduct and as a warning to them. They, the scribes and Pharisees, are like the guests who made light of the invitation and would not accept it. Hence, he tells them, God has called the poor and outcasts and has offered them the salvation which you have rejected—that is why Jesus busies himself with the latter.

St. Matthew (22, 1-14) has given us the same parable but in a different dress and with notable retouches and additions:

1. And later Jesus spoke to them once more in parables. 2. It is the case with the kingdom of heaven as with a king who was celebrating his son's marriage. 3. He sent out his servants to summon the people who had been invited to the wedding; but they refused to come. 4. Again he sent other servants to whom he said: "Tell the guests that I have prepared my banquet; my bullocks and fatted calves have been killed and all is ready. Come to the wedding." 5. But they took no notice and went off, one to his farm, another to his business. 6. While the rest, seizing the servants, maltreated them and killed them. 7. The king was furious and sent out his troops who destroyed the murderers and burned down their town. 8. Then he said to his servants: "The wedding-feast is ready, but the guests have proved unworthy. 9. Go out to the street corners and call anyone you see to the wedding." 10. The servants went out into the streets and collected all they could find, both good and bad, and the banquet-hall was full of guests.

11. When the king came in to see the guests he found one man there who was not dressed for a wedding. 12. "My friend," he said, "how do you come to be here without wedding clothes?" The man had nothing to say for himself. 13. Then the king said to his stewards: "Bind him hand and foot and cast him into the darkness outside, where there will be weeping and gnashing of teeth." 14. For many are called, but few are chosen.

Here the dinner party has become the wedding feast of a king's son—a typical elaboration of the details of a story that is constantly being retold—and, appropriately, there are many servants. Apart from this, and the new development in verses 6-7, the parable is substantially the same as that of Luke—at least as far as verse 10. For the moment we are going to forget about the second part (verses 11-14) for the good reason that, as we shall see, this does not belong to the parable of *The Feast* at all.

When we turn again to verses 1-10, and look at them more closely, we find that Luke's parable has become an allegory, a fact which is accentuated by the addition we have noticed. Verses 6-7 (the murder of the king's servants and its sequel) are not in Luke and in Matthew they break the link between verses 5 and 8, for verse 8 does follow logically on verse 5. In verse 4 we are told that the "bullocks and fatted calves have been killed and all is ready" and then we have the incongruity that the king went off on a campaign while the entire feast stood ready. He tells his servants so in verse 8 (though they had already been murdered!) for it is manifestly the same wedding feast and these are the same servants. It is evident that verses 6-7 are a later addition and refer, beyond any doubt, to the persecution and martyrdom of prophets and Christian preachers and to the destruction of Jerusalem. The Church has, as it were, brought the message up to date, for the insertion, though literally somewhat awkward, is decidedly within the scope of the parable.

With the introduction of these verses the details become significant or, more accurately, the allegorical picture is filled out: the king is God, the wedding feast is messianic blessedness, the king's son is the Messiah, the messengers are the prophets and the Apostles, the guests who ignore the invitation and maltreat the servants are the Jews, the burned city is Jerusalem and those who are called are the pagans. Since we have seen that in Luke the parable is a manifest warning to the scribes and Pharisees that their place is to be given to others, it is apparent that Matthew's allegorization serves to underline that same warning and to show its historical fulfillment in the actual rejection of the Messiah. In other words, the evangelist has adapted the parable to keep pace with events.

St. Matthew already had a model in the parable of *The Wicked Vinedressers* (21, 33-46) which, as spoken by our Lord, is strongly allegorical. But it is noteworthy that the allegorical features which occur here—and the same is true of the gospel parables generally—are almost always familiar figures from the Old Testament. God can be represented by a father, king, householder, vineyard owner. Sons, servants, vineyard and flock are the people of God. The messianic age is represented by feast or wedding and the harvest is the judgment, the "day of the Lord." These and other such traditional symbols would have been easily understood by the first hearers of the parables. When these themes do occur they are, of course, significant and so it is apparent that our Lord did not draw a rigid line between parable and allegory, and he was followed in this by the early Christians. But both he and they remained within the field of traditional symbolism and even, in very great measure, within the range of Old Testament imagery. We would be well-advised to respect those limits if we wish to interpret the parables correctly.

The Wedding Garment

We are not yet quite done with St. Matthew's treatment of *The Great Feast* and must now take up his concluding verses (11-14). We have already remarked that verses 11-13 do not belong to the parable of the Feast at all but are really another parable, or part of one. In its present context the fact that the king expected all those who had been hastily, almost forcibly, gathered in from the highways and byways to have had wedding garments has always raised a difficulty. The suggestion that the guests were presented with the garments is simply an evasion; there is no evidence of any such custom and the whole tenor of the passage implies that the guest was expected to have come properly dressed for the wedding.

Another difficulty is that the servants (*douloi*) of verses 2-10 have suddenly in verse 13 become stewards (*diakonoi*). Altogether, it is sufficiently obvious that they have to do with another parable, one concerned with the conditions of entry into the kingdom of God. Two parables have been fused[4] and it is not hard, in the present case, to realize why this has been done. The wedding

garment was meant to explain a phrase in verse 10 that could lead to misunderstanding: the servants called all they met, "both good and *bad*," and the banquet-hall was filled. Are the bad also to have a place in the kingdom of God?
—there must be some process of selection. Hence the addition of the other parable, for the moral of it is the same as that of *The Weed* (Matt. 13, 24-30) and *The Net* (13, 47f). The phrase, of course, simply means "everybody" and would have caused no trouble at all in the context of the original parable—if it had occurred in Luke, for instance. It is only when the parable had become an allegory (and all the details became more significant) that the difficulty arose, and then some explanation was demanded.

We still have to deal with verse 14 and that brings us to yet another procedure in the application of parables. It must be admitted that this verse does not fit its context very precisely. "Many are called, but few are chosen" is certainly not the moral of verses 11-13 for here the many are chosen and one only is rejected. It does not suit the first parable any better for the chosen ones are at least as numerous as those who had refused the invitation: "and the banquet-hall was full of guests." The verse is a saying of our Lord that circulated free of its context and it turns up here in view of the phrase "good and bad" for it does imply a selection. It forms an additional conclusion—a matter that needs to be explained more fully. But first it would be well to wind up our study of *The Great Feast*.

The parable of the feast as spoken by our Lord

and presented to us by St. Luke was addressed to the Pharisees and religious leaders (Luke 14, 1): they had rejected the kingdom of God, it was to be given to the poor and sinners. In certain circles of the early Church (in certain circles because Luke's source had preserved the tradition unchanged) this parable was allegorized. It was applied to Christians of the period and then additions were made to it, both to accentuate the allegorical sense and to answer some difficulties that had arisen when the details had become significant. It is not easy to determine what, in all this process, is due to the tradition and what to the evangelist. Probably, St. Matthew found the parables already fused. The insertion of verses 6-7 is most probably his work and it was very likely he who added verse 14. But in making any additions he was witness to a procedure that had been carried on from the beginning.

Secondary Conclusions

What do the parables mean? What message do they have for Christians? These were questions that occupied the mind of the primitive Church, questions that have persisted to our day. We have seen that the allegorizing method was one answer. Another and much simpler manner of applying the parables is met with frequently in the gospels: a certain number of parables have been fitted with additional conclusions which indicate the line of interpretation or manifest some special preoccupation.

The parable of *The Wicked Vinedressers*

(Mark 12, 1-11; Matt. 21, 33-46; Luke 20, 9-19) is rounded off by a quotation from Psalm 117, on the theme of the stone which was first rejected and then exalted (verses 22-23). This image does not harmonize with that of the vine and it does not fit the parable. Whereas the psalm-text was a favorite one in early Christian preaching and was used with reference to the Easter triumph of Christ (Acts 4, 11; I Pet. 2, 4, 7), the parable is aimed at the Jewish leaders and is meant to show them their guilt in plotting the death of Christ. There is no motive for mentioning the Resurrection. We may conclude that the psalm-text is no part of the original parable but has been added to it in the tradition. The reason for the addition is not difficult to find: the early Church could not speak of the death of Christ without proclaiming his resurrection.[5] In this case the meaning of the parable remains unchanged, but the presence of the psalm-text can cause some difficulty if we do not realize that it is a later addition.

A more common tendency was to add conclusions to the parable in the form of generalizing sayings. We have met one of these already at the close of *The Great Feast* (Matt. 22, 14). Just such concluding statement, which has troubled the interpretation of a parable, is that added to *The Laborers in the Vineyard* (Matt. 20, 16; *cf.* 19, 30): "Thus the last shall be first and the first last." It is noteworthy that the saying occurs independently of the parable in Mark 10, 31 and Luke 13, 30. St. Matthew has made the addition in order that a parable which Jesus had aimed at his critics would now apply to the rejection of Israel in the sense of Matt. 8, 11-12; 21, 31f. Other examples of such secondary conclusions are Matt. 25, 13 at the end of *The Ten Virgins* and a whole string of sayings (16, 9-13) added by St. Luke to *The Unjust Steward*.

Where such conclusions are found they are secondary in their present context and generally have the effect of giving the parable a wider application. This does not mean that they are not genuine sayings of our Lord but it does mean that they were not spoken by him as the conclusion of a parable. Once we have recognized them for what they are we can arrive at a better understanding of the parables concerned since, by their addition, the emphasis has usually been shifted. In most cases the result has been that a sharp warning or threat has been given a wider and less urgent moralizing bent. For example, *The Laborers in the Vineyard,* which is a defense of the gospel against its critics, has, through a new conclusion ("the last shall be first and the first last"), been transformed into an instruction about degrees of importance in the kingdom of heaven.

In these secondary conclusions we detect the hand of the Christian teacher or of an evangelist. It is understandable, indeed inevitable, that these teachers should have busied themselves in the interpretation of our Lord's message. The parables were spoken by Jesus in the context of his ministry but the Church wished to find, in these same parables, teaching for her needs—and the situation had changed radically since the Resurrection; it was necessary that the parables should be re-interpreted or, at least, re-applied to the new situation. Among other ways, this was accomplished by treating them as allegories and by adding to them apposite sayings of our Lord and thereby bringing about a shift of emphasis. Our awareness of these factors must color our approach to the parables.

What we must recognize is that the parables have a twofold historical setting. The original setting, of all the sayings of Jesus and obviously of the parables too, is a precise, concrete occasion in the life and activity of Jesus. But then, afterwards, these same parables, living words, were woven into the life of the early Church. The first Christians did not collect and treasure them merely as memorable sayings of their revered Master: they took them as addressed to themselves; they sought in them a rule of life and found in them the meaning of the Christian life. This is the second historical setting of the parables—in the situation of the primitive Church. Now we know the parables only in that form which they received within the primitive Church, and if we wish really to understand them we will want to look behind that form to the first setting, and recover their original form insofar as that is possible. Only then can we hope to hear, beyond the evangelist and the tradition, the *ipsissima vox* of Jesus.

3
The Setting
of the Parables

In the previous chapter we have indicated that many of our Lord's parables have two settings. He spoke them in a given, concrete moment of his ministry but, very often, in the early Church, they were adapted to fit the new situation after the Resurrection and to meet the needs of the first Christians. This tendency is so very natural that we today, in seeking a message for ourselves, can miss the original import of a parable even when it stares us in the face. We believe that the second part of our study will show that this does happen.

The Laborers in the Vineyard

As they now stand in the gospels, many of the parables are addressed to the disciples. When, however, we examine them more closely, we find that a high proportion of these would originally have been spoken to the crowd or to opponents. This is one very obvious manifestation of the tendency we have noted earlier: to find in the

39

parables a message for Christian living. *The Laborers in the Vineyard* (Matt. 20, 1-16) affords a good example of the frequently occurring procedure due to a change of audience.

1. It is the case with the kingdom of heaven as with a householder who went out in the early morning to hire laborers for his vineyard. 2. After agreeing with the laborers for a denarius a day, he sent them into his vineyard. 3. And going out about nine o'clock he saw others standing idle in the market-place; 4. and to them he said, "You go into my vineyard too, and I will pay you whatever is just." So they went. 5. And going out again about noon, and about three o'clock, he did the same. 6. But about five o'clock he went and found others standing; and he said to them, "Why do you stand here idle all day?" 7. "Because," they said to him, "no one has hired us." He said to them, "You also go into the vineyard."

8. And when evening came, the owner of the vineyard said to his steward, "Call the laborers and pay them their wages, beginning with the last up to the first." 9. And when those hired about five o'clock came, each of them received a denarius. 10. So when the earliest-hired came, they expected that they would receive more, but each of them also received a denarius. 11. And on receiving it they grumbled at the master: 12. "These last comers worked only one hour and yet you have put them on an equal footing with us who have borne the burden of the day and the scorching heat." 13. But

he replied to one of them, "My good fellow, I am doing you no wrong; did we not agree on a denarius? 14. Take what is yours and go. I choose to give as much to this last comer as to you: 15. have I not the right to do what I like with my own goods? Or are you envious because I am good?"

16. So the last will be first and the first last; [for many are called, but few are chosen].

The passage forms the gospel of the Mass on Septuagesima Sunday. In this liturgical setting it is manifestly interpreted as a call to God's Vineyard; but that is to miss the point of the conclusion which shows that the emphasis does not lie on a call to the vineyard but on the distribution of wages at the day's end. This much is true, in general, but then, we may ask, what precisely is the conclusion? Most of the gospel manuscripts read as the second part of verse 16: "For many are called but few are chosen." How does the parable illustrate the truth that many hear the invitation but few only attain salvation?— for it has often been interpreted thus. In this view those who were first employed are presented as a warning: they are called but, because of their murmuring, they cut themselves off from salvation. There can be no doubt that this is a misinterpretation of the parable for the workers in question are not rejected but receive the agreed wage just the same as the others. We should note, moreover, that the saying is missing in some important Greek manuscripts and in certain versions, and is almost certainly a later addition.

But even if it were authentic, it is nothing other than a generalization—it also occurs in 22, 14—and must be ignored if we are to arrive at the original meaning of the parable.

The first part of verse 16 still remains: "But many that are first will be last and the last first" —does this point to the meaning? It would concern the equality of reward in the Kingdom of God: there is no difference, all are equal. Quite apart from the fact that such teaching is highly doubtful, to say the least, it can be shown that it is not the moral of the parable.

It is significant that the saying is found again not only in 19, 30 but also in Mark 10, 31 and Luke 13, 30; in other words, it is an independent and floating logion added to the parable as a secondary conclusion. We can even see why it was added. Verse 8b: "Call the laborers and pay them their wages, beginning with the last up to the first" seemed to represent a reversal of rank that would take place at the judgment and the saying would appear to be perfectly in place. But it is so only at first sight because the wage is still the same in each case and the mere order in which it is handed out can make very little difference. Besides, verse 8b may be rendered quite accurately: "Pay them their wages, including the last as well as the first."[1] So, in all respects, verse 16 is obviously secondary in its context and should not be taken into account if we wish to recover the sense of the parable as it was spoken by our Lord.

The parable, then, originally ended at verse 15 and the key to it is the last phrase of the verse: "because I am good." It is this goodness that explains the apparently capricious conduct of the householder. For, indeed, at first sight, it does seem unfair that all the workers were to receive the same wage. But when we understand the motive we judge his action very differently. A denarius represented a day's wage, just enough to support a family; anything less, and especially the payment for one hour, would be quite inadequate. It is because he had pity on them that the owner called them to the vineyard in the first place and it is because he has pity on them that he pays all a full wage. There is nothing arbitrary in his conduct—it is the action of a man who is full of compassion for the poor. So, too, does God act, for God is all goodness and mercy: this is the message of the parable.

But if we look at it more closely again we shall see that it is two-pronged, that it is made up of two episodes. First we have the hiring of the laborers and the instruction about their payment (verses 1-8) and then follows the indignation of the recipients who feel themselves injured (verses 9-15). Now, it is characteristic of two-pronged parables that the emphasis falls on the second point and if this is so we must realize that the parable is meant for people who resemble the murmurers; the gospels make it abundantly clear that the Pharisees fit the bill. The good news was addressed to publicans and sinners precisely because God had taken pity on them, poor and helpless as they were; that is why Jesus seeks them out. And these legally minded men cavil at him because he is a friend of these despised ones, these outcasts. In this parable he faces up to his critics and defends his gospel. He shows them what God is like, full of compassion for the poor, and he points out to them how wrong it is that they should be scandalized at his great goodness.

Surely, it is readily understandable that Christians were not too interested in this scandal of the Pharisees. They sought a message for their own lives in all the words of Christ and they took this parable, too, as addressed to themselves. This is its second setting, in the life of the primitive Church. Its teaching was not thereby falsified, but the change of audience necessarily involved a shift of emphasis and the new application was achieved by such means as the secondary conclusion of verse 16.

The Lost Sheep

In chapter 15 of his gospel St. Luke has grouped three parables, all of them addressed to those who criticized and opposed the good news preached—in word and deed—by Jesus. We have just seen that this is not unusual but is rather a feature of the gospels. Time and again we have the charge brought against him that he rubs shoulders with publicans and sinners, that he is the champion of the outcast. Even so, we may be surprised to realize just how many of his parables were spoken in defense of his own conduct. In these parables Jesus points out to the Pharisees the unbounded goodness of God and strives to bring them to a realization of the fact that they, by their critical and unsympathetic attitude, are setting themselves up as judges of God's ways.

According to St. Luke, the parable of the *Lost Sheep* was occasioned by the Pharisees' complaint: "This man welcomes sinners and even eats with them" (15, 2). In reply, Jesus tells of the shepherd who went in search of the sheep that was lost and of his joy when he had found the stray. There can be no missing the moral of the story: "Even so, I tell you, God[2] will have more joy over one sinner who repents than over ninety-nine persons who need no repentance" (15, 7). Quietly, but unmistakably, the critics are told that they are being utterly unreasonable, that, in fact, they are presuming to question the mercy of God. Jesus says to them: "Just as the shepherd, when he has gathered his flock into his fold, rejoices over the sheep which he has found at last, so God rejoices over the repentant sinner: he rejoices because he can forgive. That is why I receive sinners."[3]

The same parable occurs in Matthew. Here it is no longer addressed to the critics of the good news but to the disciples; it forms part of the discourse that begins: "Thus it is not the will of your heavenly Father that one of these little ones should perish" (18, 14). Even if the application were not already clear the context clinches the issue because the warning not to despise one of the least (verse 10) and the admonition regarding fraternal correction (verses 15-17) leave no doubt about the interpretation of verse 14: "It is God's will that you should go after your erring brother—the 'little one', weak and helpless—as earnestly as the shepherd of the parable sought out the lost sheep."[4]

It is evident that St. Luke has preserved the original setting of the parable, but the change of audience evident in Matthew is very easily explained. The early Christians sought in this, as in other parables, a message that fitted their own needs and so they interpreted it as applying to themselves. In acting thus they have not forced its message. *The Lost Sheep* was spoken to justify the concern shown by Jesus for sinners and outcasts; the Christian, if he is to be like his Master, must manifest great solicitude for his erring brother, one who has wandered out of the fold and gone straying from the flock. The ultimate result is a shift of emphasis: an apologetic parable has taken on a hortatory character.

The Talents

The Lost Sheep is no isolated example and many parables have been similarly transformed. They have lost their original *Sitz im Leben* ("setting in life") and found a new setting in the life of the early Church. We may further illustrate this phenomenon by studying the parable of *The Talents* (Matt. 25, 14-30) and by comparing it with *The Pounds* (Luke 19, 12-27).

14. It is as when a man about to go abroad called his servants and entrusted to them his property; 15. to one he gave five talents, to another two and to a third one— to each according to his ability—and took his departure. 16. He who had received the five talents went at once and traded with

them, and made five more. 17. And likewise he who had received the two made two more. 18. But he who had received the one went off and dug a hole in the ground, and hid his master's money.

19. Now after a long time the master of those servants returned and settled accounts with them. 20. And he who had received the five talents came forward bringing five talents more: "Master," he said, "you entrusted me with five talents; see, I have made five talents more!" 21. His master said to him: "Well done, good and faithful servant; you have been faithful over a little, I will set you over much. Enter into the joy of your lord." 22. Then he also who had the two talents came forward: "Master," he said, "you delivered to me two talents; see, I have made two talents more!" 23. His master said to him: "Well done, good and faithful servant; you have been faithful over a little, I will set you over much. Enter into the joy of your lord." 24. Finally, he who had received the one talent came forward: "Master," he said, "I knew you to be a hard man, reaping where you did not sow and gathering where you did not winnow, so I was afraid and went and hid your talent in the ground. See—here you have what is yours." 26. But his master answered him: "You wicked and indolent servant! You knew that I reap where I have not sown and gather where I have not winnowed? 27. In that case you ought to have invested my money with the bankers, then, on my return, I should have re-

ceived my own with interest. 28. So take the talent away from him, and give it to him who has the ten talents."

29. "For to every one who has will more be given, and he will have abundance; but from him who has not, even what he has will be taken away. 30. And cast that useless servant into the outer darkness: there shall be the weeping and the gnashing of teeth."

Matthew has placed the parable in the last of the five discourses of his gospel—the eschatological discourse. In that context it has to do with the second coming of the Son of Man and it stands as a warning to the disciples of Christ that at his coming he will take account of the manner in which they had made use of the gifts they had received and of the opportunities that had been presented to them.

The eschatological note is very clear in the phrase: "enter into the joy of your lord" (verses 21, 23) for "joy" really stands for "joyous feast" —the Messianic Banquet. And the closing verse, 30, clearly refers to the Last Judgment. Significantly, this verse occurs elsewhere in Matthew: 8, 12; 22, 13; cf. 13, 42.50; 24, 51. And, indeed when we look at the parable more closely, we shall realize that it originally had a different import.

The parable of *The Pounds* (Luke 19, 12-27) will be treated below in some detail. Here it will suffice to remark that its present form is the result of a fusion of two parables, for the verses 12.14. 17.19.27 would seem to come from another parable which we might name *The Pretender*. If we admit this (there is really not much doubt about it) then *The Pounds* and *The Talents* are fundamentally the same—two versions of one parable. Details have been changed, of course: the three servants of Matthew become ten in Luke but, on the other hand, the sum entrusted to them is very much smaller.

We might reconstruct the common story along these lines: a man summoned his servants, gave them sums of money in trust and went away. When he returned he called them to account. All, except one, had notably increased the capital and were commended. The remaining one admitted that he had been unwilling to risk losing the money and had carefully hidden it. Now he produces it and, no doubt, expects to be commended in his turn for his prudence. Instead he is soundly berated for his inexcusable lack of enterprise—he might at least have gotten interest on the money. As it is, the sum he had received is taken from him and given to another.

It is evident that the parable is primarily concerned with the action of the cautious servant—the others serve as foils to him. We may well ask who this servant is who had buried the talent given to him, or had hidden the money in a napkin; since the money belonged to another his action amounted to a breach of trust. What class of people might our Lord have had in mind? It cannot be doubted that the parable was addressed to the religious leaders, to the scribes especially. Elsewhere Jesus had said openly of these: "Woe to you lawyers! for you have taken away the key of knowledge; you did not enter yourselves, and you hindered those who were entering" (Luke 11, 52).

To apply to them the sentence passed on the unprofitable servant is merely a change of metaphor. They had been entrusted with a great treasure: God's word. But, through a policy of selfish exclusiveness, they had made the religion of Israel barren. "Simple folk, publicans and sinners, Gentiles, have no benefit from the Pharisaic observance of the Law, and God has no interest on his capital."[5] They had failed in their trust. The parable was meant to bring them to recognize their conduct, to see it in its true light; to bring them to the realization that the gift God had given them was not for themselves alone. They were called upon to be enterprising, to take a risk. Because they did nothing but selfishly kept that treasure for themselves, they stood condemned. *The Talents* is one of the many parables which Jesus always striving to open their eyes addressed to the leaders of the people; this is its *Sitz im Leben.*

With the founding of the Church the role of the scribes was over, they were no longer the custodians of God's word. The early Christians were not very interested in what our Lord had to say to that obsolete class but they were passionately interested in what his words might mean for them. Therefore, it would seem, they gave to the parable of *The Talents* its widest application by adding the maxim: "To every one who has will God give; from him who has not will he take away what he has" (*cf.* Matt. 25, 29; Mark 4, 25;

Luke 19, 26). The parable at this point has to do with the absolute freedom of God in regard to his gifts. Matthew's grading of the amounts of money entrusted to the three servants is a further modification to illustrate the variety of human endowments. In fact it is in this way that the parable is commonly understood: each of us has received one or more "talents" and we are expected to put them to good use.

Soon a new preoccupation brought about a fresh interpretation of the parable, one that was to mark it profoundly. It had become apparent to the early Christians that the *parousia,* the second coming of Christ, would be delayed and they began to read *The Talents* in the light of his frequent warnings to keep awake and prepared, for he would come "like a thief in the night." In Matthew the master is seen as the Son of Man himself, and his reckoning with his servants has become the Last Judgment. Luke, in his introduction, makes explicit the application to the second coming: "He proceeded to tell a parable because he was near to Jerusalem and because they supposed that the kingdom of God was to appear immediately" (19, 11). And, by adding details from another parable, he describes Christ as ascending to heaven in order to return as king.

Although, for convenience, we have referred these last modifications to St. Matthew and St. Luke it is indeed probable that the evangelists had found the developments in their sources. Be that as it may, it is at least clear that the changing interests of the early Church brought about changes in interpretation. In the process not only

has the original parable been modified in details
(the differences of *The Talents* and *The Pounds*)
but the setting has been altered completely and
the new interpretations have been worked out
by the familiar methods of secondary conclusion
and allegorization. And the surprising result of
it all is that, though the audience has changed
and though the interest is different, the teaching
remains very much that of the original parable;
indeed, this teaching has been underlined more
urgently. Christians, too, are entrusted with a
great treasure—they are expected to bear fruit
(John 15, 2) and their Master will hold a reckoning.

By way of conclusion we may be permitted to
point once again to a factor that must be kept in
mind: many of the parables have a twofold setting. The form in which they have come to us,
via the tradition and the evangelists, may not be
the form which Jesus gave them; it is even more
likely that the audience has changed. Of course,
we do not make this observation with regret or
mark it down as loss. Any change that has come
about, in the parables as in all the sayings of
Jesus, has been wrought within the Church of
Christ and under the guidance of his Spirit. But
just because the purpose of this book is to win
back to the *ipsissima verba* of the Lord—or to
indicate how this may be done—we do look beyond the evangelist and the tradition, not with
disdain, but simply because we would hear *his*
words. And to achieve this—as nearly as possible
—we must determine what the Germans call the
Sitz im Leben Jesu of the parables, their concrete,

historical setting in the ministry of our Lord. If we do succeed in this, in some measure, an inevitable result will be a deeper understanding of the parables. And the example of the first Christians, so manifest in the gospels, will surely spur us to build our Christian lives, as they did, on the words of the Master because no matter to whom they may be addressed, these remain words of eternal life for us as for them.

4

The Message
of the Parables

In his parables Jesus has given the very stuff of his gospel, and these parables speak a language that must strike a chord in the heart of every man. But one who really wants to understand them, to savor the rich marrow of them, will strive to determine their setting in the life and ministry of Jesus. We have tried to show the feasibility of this attempt, to illustrate the immense profit that follows even limited success, but it must be obvious that, in three short chapters, we can have hastily sketched the process—no more. The present chapter, by way of conclusion, indicates in general lines the original message of the parables, before they had been applied and adapted by the Church. Thus we are able to stand as close as possible to the Master, seeking to catch his very accents. And though we must feel that we still miss a great deal, our verdict will be, beyond any shadow of doubt: "Never has man spoken like this man!" (John 7, 46).

The Kingdom

Christ came on earth to found a kingdom, the kingdom of God. Although, in his plan, it had already dawned, for it was present in him and in his work, it was to develop until the end of time. It had come quietly, however, so quietly that men had missed its coming. Yet, henceforth, it is a reality and no power on earth can hinder its development because it is livened by the power of God. In many of his parables Jesus has taught men about his kingdom.

A parable like that of *The Mustard Seed* must be viewed in the setting of the Galilean ministry. It was a time of promise, but a keen observer could sense, behind the enthusiasm of the crowds, a lurking doubt, a disenchantment that would spread and deepen. Already, too, the bitter opposition of the ruling classes was evident. And the little band of disciples, insignificant men— could that be the cradle of any hope for the future? The parable, however, lifts a corner of the veil, and the wisdom of men is confounded.

> With what can we compare the kingdom of God, or by what parable shall we describe it? It is the case with it as with a grain of mustard seed . . . (Mark 4, 30f).

Our Lord admits that the kingdom, in its beginnings, gives no obvious promise of its range, no more than a tiny seed seems capable of growing into a tall shrub. But from that seed a tree does spring, offering its branches as shelter to the birds; and from the little band of Jesus' disciples a kingdom will grow, spreading wide and embracing all men. In the world—to look at it another way—that kingdom will be like leaven in a mass of dough (Luke 13, 20f), a restless ferment transforming the world, a vital reality that the world cannot ignore.

The marvelous growth of the kingdom is the work of God; this is the lesson of *The Seed Growing Secretly*:

> It is with the kingdom of God as with a man who has scattered seed upon the ground: whether he sleeps or rises, night or day, the seed sprouts and grows—he knows not how. Of itself the earth produces first the blade, then the ear, then the full grain in the ear. And when the grain is ripe, at once he puts in the sickle because the harvest has come. (Mark 4, 26-29).

The little seed of the kingdom has within it, implanted there by God, its own principle of growth, an intimate and irresistible force, which will bring it to fulfillment. St. Paul had learned the lesson of the parable: "I planted, Appollos watered, but God gave the growth" (I Cor. 3, 6). Moreover, God lets things run their course. Weeds will grow together with the good grain until the harvest time (Matt. 13, 24-30) and the wide-cast net of the fishers of men will enclose some who prove unworthy (13, 47f). That is God's way of doing things—he will bring about the separation of good and bad in his own time.

In the parable of *The Sower* (Mark 4, 3-8 parr.) we are shown the harvest of the kingdom, a harvest abundant beyond expectations; the seed has grown despite weeds and birds and inhospitable soil. Jesus encourages his disciples, telling them that in spite of every failure and every hindrance, the kingdom of God grows and develops. He gives them the assurance that they can trust God absolutely, an assurance brought home to them by the related parables of *The Unjust Judge* (Luke 18, 28) and *The Friend at Midnight* (11, 5-8).

The lesson of *The Unjust Judge* is explicit: "And will not God vindicate his elect who cry to him day and night? I tell you he will vindicate them speedily" (18, 7f). Although St. Luke has used the parable to illustrate persevering prayer, it is evident that, in its original context, the emphasis is not on the entreaties of the widow but on the action of the judge. Only the Son could so boldly draw a parallel between this inconsiderate man and the Father.

In *The Friend at Midnight,* our Lord stressed the action of the friend who is within, not the persistence of the other. This becomes obvious once we have realized that the phrase: "Which of you?" — *tis ex humon* — (11, 5) regularly, in the New Testament, introduces questions which invite the emphatic answer: "Impossible!", "Nobody!" or "Of course!", "Everyone!"[1] The phrase may best be rendered: "Can you imagine that any of you would . . .?" In the passage in question verses 5-7 should be regarded as one long rhetorical question: "Can you imagine that if one of you had a friend, and he should come to you at midnight and say to you, 'Friend, lend me three loaves, for a friend of mine on a journey has come to me and I have nothing to set before him, that you would answer, 'Go away and leave me in peace'—can you imagine that?" The answer must be an indignant denial: "Impossible!"; "Of course not!"[2]

The lesson, made explicit in verse 8, is clear: If the friend, though roused in the middle of the night, yet without a moment's hesitation helps out his neighbor (the oriental code of hospitality is at stake), how much more will God hasten to the aid of those who call upon him. The children of the kingdom have this assurance that God does listen to them, that God will help them.

The Crisis

Our Lord proclaimed the coming of the kingdom, the day of salvation, but he also sounded a call to repentance in view of the terrible urgency of the hour. Again and again he raised his voice in warning, earnestly striving to open the eyes of a blind people. Many of his parables have this object in view.

The little parable of *The Capricious Children* (Matt. 11, 16f, Luke 7, 31f) is his sad comment on an irresponsible generation: they are no better than children. As always, the sketch is drawn from life. Jesus recalls the children he had seen in many a village of Galilee playing at weddings (the boys) and funerals (the girls)[3]—as another was stirred by the memory of children "playing on the streets of little towns in Connaught." But for all its charm "the picture of petulant children who quarrel about their games suggests the frivolous captiousness of a generation who would not see that the movement inaugurated by John and brought to such an unexpected pitch by Jesus was a crisis of the first magnitude, but wasted their time in foolish carping at the asceticism of the one, and the good-companionship of the other. They fiddled while Rome was burning."[4]

But most of these parables are addressed to a definite class—the scribes and Pharisees. Indeed, one important result of studying the parables in their original context is that it leads us to an awareness of our Lord's great solicitude for these blind guides. He sought by every means to open their eyes, for he had come that they too might have life—if they would.

The parable of *The Talents* sounds a warning to the leaders of the people (Matt. 25, 14-30).[5] As it now stands in Matthew its lesson is that Christians are servants whom their Master has entrusted with gifts to be employed for the development of his kingdom; he will demand of them an account of their stewardship. But this is a Christian application of a parable addressed by Jesus to the Pharisees. As he spoke it the emphasis fell on the conduct of the third servant: this "wicked and slothful servant" stood for the Pharisee who hid under a bushel the light God had given him and who had kept selfishly for himself the gift that was meant for mankind. The Pharisees, as a class, were extremely nationalistic and exclusive, but the time is at hand when God will settle accounts with those who so abuse his gifts.

In one last appeal to the Jewish leaders, Jesus held the mirror up to them and showed them their true selves. *The Wicked Vinedressers* (Mark 12, 1-9; Matt. 21, 33-41; Luke 20, 9-16) is very nearly an allegory. In the Old Testament, Israel is God's vineyard (*cf.* Isa. 5, 1-7) and God's prophets are his "servants" (*cf.* Amos 3, 7), and in these traditional images the parable gives an outline of God's solicitude for his people and of their ingratitude. Then Jesus reveals to them what they, more wicked than their fathers, already intended in their hearts to do. Perhaps the manifestation of his awareness of their evil purpose will shock them to their senses—otherwise they will be destroyed and the Vineyard given to others. "In a sense, the tale was autobiography; the Man who told it was its central figure; and within a few days of his telling it, it came true. God sent his 'only son' to Israel, making his last appeal; and they slew him, on an April day, outside the northern wall of Jerusalem."[6]

God's Mercy for Sinners

The parables of crisis do not exhaust the list of those addressed to the scribes and Pharisees. It may, at first sight, seem incongruous that the best known and best loved parables were spoken to that same unsympathetic audience. When Jesus declares so emphatically that the salvation he brings is for the *poor* and that he has come as a Savior of *sinners,* he is not preaching to the poor and to sinners—these he seeks out and gathers to him; for them he himself is the sermon that has won them. When he speaks of his great solicitude he is on the defensive, he is justifying his gospel, he is vindicating the honor of a loving God. The parables concerned with the very heart of the gospel are, it seems without exception, not addressed to simple, goodwilled folk but to the critics of the gospel. This is their distinctive character, their *Sitz im Leben*.

Jesus took different lines of approach in the vindication of his gospel. In a whole series of parables he turned the eyes of his critics on the poor to whom he preached the good news. The tone of these is set, and their context indicated, in a declaration which he once made in answer to a specific charge:

> The scribes of the Pharisee party, when they saw that he ate with sinners and publicans, said to his disciples: "Why does he eat with publicans and sinners?" Jesus, who had heard the question, said to them: "Those who are healthy have no need of a doctor, but those who are sick. I have not come to call the just, but sinners" (Mark 3, 16f, parr.).

The Two Sons (Matt. 21, 28-31) teaches the lesson very pointedly; it dramatizes the judgment that Jesus has passed on the Pharisees: "they preach, but do not practice" (Matt. 23, 3). It is those who have hitherto been deaf to God's call and blind to his law who will now at last listen and obey: "Amen I say to you, the publicans and the harlots go into the kingdom before you" (21, 31). St. Luke's parable of *The Two Debtors* (7, 41f) makes the same point, but this time in terms of individuals. Simon is bluntly told that the woman whom he despised is nearer to God than he.

Our Lord also asks his critics to look at themselves and in that process he hands out to them a stern rebuke. They are like the guests who disdainfully declined the invitation to the feast, and then looked with contempt on those who had taken their places (Luke 14, 16-24; Matt. 22, 1-10). They are like the vinedressers who arrogantly insulted their Lord and maltreated his servants. They are those who have already chosen for themselves the best places in the kingdom; but they are warned that God's assessment of their worth may not equate with the opinion they have formed of themselves—they may be lucky to be offered even the lowest place, (Luke 14, 7-11).

Most decisively of all, it is in parables like *The Prodigal Son* (Luke 15, 11-32) that Jesus vindicated his bringing of the good news to the despised and outcast. It is because God eagerly desires the repentance of sinners that Jesus associates with them, he wants to win them back to God. The Pharisees are like the elder son who grumbled at his father's generosity; they are scandalized by the ways of God, his great love. The other parables of chapter 15 of Luke—*The Lost Sheep* (3-7) and *The Lost Coin* (8-10)—likewise justify the concern of our Lord for sinners and outcasts.

The Laborers in the Vineyard (Matt. 20, 1-16) served the same purpose, though this aspect is now obscured by the secondary conclusion of verse 16. This parable is two-pronged: (1) the hiring of the laborers (1-8); (2) the indignation of the first-comers (9-15) and, characteristically, the emphasis falls on the second point. Although it seems arbitrary, the conduct of the vineyard owner is really not so, and he is being criticized unfairly. Out of the goodness of his heart he pays all, even the latest comers, a full day's wage; he thinks not only of them but of their families and knows that the wage of a single hour would be altogether inadequate. The final words, "because I am good" (verse 15) give the key to the parable; it was obviously addressed to those who resembled the murmurers, to those who criticized the good news and opposed it.

Jesus did associate with sinners, he did seek them out, and he did win them over. All this the self-righteous critics could not understand. And so our Lord strove to make them understand the utter unreasonableness of their point of view; he tried to make them realize the infinite value, in God's eyes, of the little ones, the sick, the straying sheep. Again and again he is faced with the question: "Why do you mix with this rabble?" Tirelessly, in these parables, he replies: "Because they are sick and need me, because they show the gratitude of children forgiven by their Father. And because, on the other hand, you do not want me, you who are loveless, self-righteous, rebellious. But above all, because God is like that: so good to the poor, so joyful when the stray is found, so full of a father's love for the returning child, so gracious to the despairing, the helpless, the needy. That is why!"[7]

Disciples

If Jesus so lovingly sought out the poor, the unfortunate, the erring, it was to transform them into disciples. Once they have turned to him, they cannot go back again to their former ways. Henceforth, he makes demands of them; they must be sons of the kingdom.

His call to those who are to be true followers of his is brought out in the twin parables of *The Hidden Treasure* and *The Pearl of Great Price* (Matt. 13, 44-46). A man must be prepared to give up everything for the sake of the kingdom— this, we have come to believe, is their message. But is the emphasis really on the cost of the surrender? After all, the men concerned are highly conscious of being the gainers. Rather, the key-words are "in his joy" (verse 44); both men are overwhelmed by the splendor of their discovery. This was the experience of one who is surely the very greatest of disciples: "I count everything as loss because of the surpassing worth of knowing Christ Jesus my Lord. For his sake I have suffered the loss of all things, and count them as refuse, in order that I may gain Christ" (Phil. 3, 8). It is clear that Paul would have gone at once to the heart of the parables.

The quality that Jesus looks for in a faithful disciple is a boundless love and in *The Good Samaritan* he has taught the lesson in a way that may not be mistaken and cannot be forgotten (Luke 10, 30-37). He implies that the lawyer's question: "Who is my neighbor?" has no place in the Christian life. True charity does not pause to consider matters of color or race or creed, but goes out without reserve to one in need. The Christian's neighbor is Everyman—his love can have no limits.

But Christian love has deeper reaches still. The true disciple, like the woman who was a sinner, is conscious of being the recipient of great mercy (Luke 7, 47) and the effect of this realization is underlined, by contrast, in *The Unmerciful Servant* (Matt. 18, 23-25). A man who has been freed of a crippling burden, who has experienced the wonder of divine forgiveness, must surely feel compelled to pardon the trifling offenses of others. "Love is not resentful . . . love bears all things" (1 Cor. 13, 5.7)—otherwise it is not love.

The End

The kingdom has come and has been established on earth, but the fulfillment is not yet. Many parables take up the classic Old Testament images of the End: judgment, harvest, feast, marriage.[8]

The end will come like a thief in the night (Matt. 24, 43-44), like a master returning unexpectedly from a long journey (Matt. 13, 34-37), like a bridegroom who tarries on the way (Matt. 25, 1-13). Then it is that the true standing of a man will be seen: the tree will be judged by its fruits (Matt. 7, 16-20), the master will demand an account of his servants (18, 23-25). Then will come the great sifting: the separation of corn and weeds (13, 24-30), of good and useless fish (13, 47-50), of wise and foolish virgins (25, 1-13), of faithful and unfaithful servants (25, 14-30). Sentence or reward will follow: the wicked, cut off from the joyful family of God (22, 11-13; 24, 45-51) will be thrown into prison (5, 25-26; 18, 23-35), cast into the fire (7, 16-20; 13, 24-30). Then, at last, the faithful will have a reward far beyond their merits (20, 1-16; 24, 45-47), the joy of the wedding-feast (22, 1-13; 20, 1-13).

At the close of this first part of our brief study we may recall the words of St. Mark: "With many such parables he spoke the word to them, as they were able to hear it" (4, 33). We should remind ourselves that he still speaks to us in these same parables, and that their message may be more or less meaningful for us as it was for their first hearers. But we can be sure that they will speak to us more plainly if we strive to know them better. And we may come to hear in them, across the centuries, the lingering echo of the *ipsissima vox* of Jesus Christ, our Lord.

PART II
THE PARABLES
OF THE
THIRD GOSPEL

5

The Kingdom Comes

In a summary statement early in his gospel St. Mark gives the burden of Jesus' initial preaching in Galilee:

> The time is completed, and the kingdom of God is at hand; repent and believe in the glad tidings (1, 15).

Our Lord, speaking of the kingdom of God, obviously takes for granted that his listeners would know what he meant. He spoke of something already familiar to them and he did not have to begin by explaining the term. In the Old Testament, however, the expression occurs only rarely and only in the later books (*e.g.* Tob. 13, 1; Ps. 145, 11-12; Dan. 3, 100; Wis. 10, 10). Yet, though the name is not prevalent, the reality of the kingdom of God is very much in evidence, and the synoptic use of the term has Old Testament roots (*e.g.* Num. 23, 21; 1 Sam. 12, 13; Isa. 52, 7; 1 Chr. 29, 11).

In the teaching of our Lord the kingdom is, first and foremost, an intervention of God in history. This is also true of the Old Testament idea, but in the New Testament view the divine intervention is made manifest in the coming of the Son of God. However, the kingdom remains a mysterious reality whose true nature Jesus alone knows. And he makes it known, not to the wise and clever, but to little ones (Luke 10, 21); the secret of the kingdom is revealed to Christ's disciples (Mark 4, 11) for to that little flock the Father has been pleased to give the kingdom (Luke 12, 32).

The essential secret of the kingdom that was impressed on this small group is that in Jesus, and in his words and works, the kingdom was already present. This is also the point that Jesus sought to put before the people at large; he tried to make it evident to their leaders. It was in his parables especially that he presented the kingdom, showing its presence and its growth, painting the dispositions of those who had come to accept it, warning those who opposed it of their dreadful plight and, at all times, urging the great love and mercy of the kingdom's King.

He preached the good news to his followers "as they were able to hear it" (Mark 4, 33). The tragedy is that so many would not listen. The parables illustrate the untiring solicitude of the Savior for some who had obstinately closed their eyes to the light: to the very end of his ministry —while they plotted his death—he tried to win them. Nothing else so dramatically sets in relief the unbounded love of our Lord. As we listen to those pleas and warnings and threats, all with one end in view, we cannot fail to share some of St. Paul's amazement before the mystery of divine goodness:

> While we were still helpless, Christ at the fitting time died for the ungodly . . . God proves his love toward us, because, while we were yet sinners, Christ died for us. (Rom. 5, 6-8).

The essential fact is that the kingdom has come. But it has come quietly, unnoticed. It is like a seed that must germinate, a plant that must spring up and grow; this seed, sown by God, will ripen to a vast harvest. And, like leaven in a mass of dough, it will permeate the world of men to the end of time.

THE SOWER
Luke 8, 4-8 (Mark 4, 1-9; Matt. 13, 1-9)

4. Now when a great crowd was gathering, and the people from every town were resorting to him, he addressed them in a parable: 5. "The sower went out to sow his seed; and as he sowed, some fell along the roadside, where it was trodden upon, and the birds of the air devoured it. 6. And some fell upon the rock; but on sprouting it withered from lack of moisture. 7. And some fell amid the briers, and the briers grew up with it and choked it. 8. And some fell upon good soil; and springing up it yielded a hundredfold crop."

The setting of the parable in Luke is quite general: Jesus is "journeying through towns and villages, preaching and proclaiming the good news of the kingdom of God" (8, 1); it is just somewhere in Galilee that he speaks the parable to an assembled crowd. Though Luke is certainly following Mark he has omitted many of the vivid details of Mark. Consider, for example, the setting: in Mark, Jesus sat in a boat and taught the people gathered on the shore.

On the other hand, Luke can make additions. Thus, in verse 5, he has added *his seed* and also that the seed *was trodden upon*. The second detail betrays the evangelist's concern to make the parable more intelligible to his Greek readers who would, of course, have been unfamiliar with Palestinian agricultural conditions. And unless we are, to some extent, aware of these conditions, the action of the sower must seem strange. In Palestine sowing precedes plowing and the sower strides over the unplowed stubble. He sows intentionally on the casual path because it is going to be plowed up—as are the withered thorns; he cannot avoid the rocks that jut through the thin soil.[1]

Luke's *rock*, for Mark's *rocky ground*, again abstracts from local conditions. He depicts the seed as falling on a roadway or on rocks bordering a field; it is surely the way that we tend to visualize the situation. It would seem that Luke's desire for simplification has led him too far because it is hard to see how seed fallen on a rock can grow or even sprout! (the "rocky ground" of Mark raises no such difficulty); yet the idea remains perfectly clear. Luke underlines the astonishing abundance of the harvest, omitting the thirtyfold and sixtyfold of Mark.

If we take the parable just as it stands, keeping in mind the Palestinian background and realizing that it was spoken by Jesus in the enthusiastic period of the Galilean ministry, the original meaning of it must surely be obvious.

On the one hand we have a description of the difficulties and frustration that meet the sower: poor land, thieving birds, scorching sun and thorns. On the other hand we are assured that, despite all this, the seed ripens to the harvest, a harvest abundant beyond expectations. In spite of everything, we are taught, in the face of every failure and of every hindrance, the kingdom of God will grow and develop. But though the idea of growth is certainly present, it does not come to the forefront, the emphasis is on the harvest. The perspective is eschatological[2] for the harvest is the full flowering of the kingdom.

EXPLANATION OF THE SOWER

Luke 8, 11-15; (Mark 4, 13-20; Matt. 13, 18-23)

11. Now the parable means this: The seed is the word of God. 12. And those along the roadside are they that have heard; then comes the devil, and takes away the word from their heart, that they may not believe and be saved. 13. And those upon the rock are they who, when they hear, receive the word with delight; yet these have no root: they believe for a while, and in the hour of trial fall away. 14. And that falling among the briers are they that have heard; yet, as

they go on their way, are choked by the
anxieties and riches and pleasures of life,
and bring no fruit to maturity. 15. But that
upon the good soil are they who, with a noble
and generous heart, having heard the word,
hold it fast, and yield fruit with endurance.

The question of the disciples and the reply of
Jesus (verses 9-10) follow Mark 4, 10-12. That
passage of Mark, and its importance for an understanding of the purpose of the gospel parables,
has been treated earlier.[3]

We have noted that the message of the parable,
in its original *Sitz im Leben,* is concerned with
the development of the kingdom: the emphasis
is on the abundant harvest. But, like many of
the parables, *The Sower* found a new setting in
the life of the early Church. The point of interest became the word, and the hearer's reception
of the word, for the Christians have applied the
parable to themselves; it has become an exhortation to converts to examine themselves and to
test the sincerity of their conversion. In order to
do this the parable has been allegorized.

Upon examination it is obvious that the explanation of *The Sower* is somewhat forced. A
study of the vocabulary confirms the impression
that it is indeed a later development; here it will
suffice to take just one example. The expression
"the word," used absolutely, is a technical term
for the gospel, one used widely in the primitive
Church (*cf.* Acts 4, 4; 6, 4; 8, 4; 10, 36, 44; etc.);
it is surely significant that "the word" is found
in the mouth of Jesus *only* in the explanation of

The Sower (eight times in Mark and, in the parallel texts, five times in Matthew and three times in Luke). Otherwise in the symbolic gospels, it occurs in four redactional passages (Mark 2, 2; 4, 33; 16, 20; Luke 1,2). And this is only one, if not the chief, point of the linguistic argument. Throughout we are dealing with the language of the Church and not with the customary manner of speech of our Lord.

It seems clear that Luke is aware that the traditional interpretation does not quite fit the parable and he does attempt to overcome the difficulty, but he can succeed only to a limited extent. By "word of God" he understands the preaching of Jesus: the seed is thus the gospel preaching. In the original parable the seed (*i.e.* the kingdom) held the center of interest throughout. In the application the emphasis is on the reaction of men to the gospel preaching, and the seed has to represent *both* the word *and* the hearers of the word. But though the details of the explanation must, in the circumstances, be strained, the explanation itself is readily understandable.

However, when we compare the text of Mark, we realize that Luke has gone a long way toward making it easier to grasp. In this connection we might note an example of how freely Luke can, at times, adapt his source. With Mark 4, 11-12 before his eyes he leaves aside the conclusion of the citation from Isaiah (6, 10): "lest they should return and their sins should be forgiven them"—yet he keeps it in mind for his addition in verse 12: "that they may not believe and be saved" is clearly an echo of it.

In the original parable the details were not significant, instead they filled in the rural background of the story, but in the allegorical application they have a symbolical value. The thieving birds represent Satan ready to snatch away the word before it can take root. In verses 13-14 the seed represents exclusively the hearers of the word—though we have to recall that in verse 11 "the seed is the word." Those standing on the rock have no root, they are hearers who will not persevere; the thorns symbolize the cares, riches and pleasures of life which eventually overcome those who grow among them.

It is to be noted that the explanation, so far, has considered only the obstacles in the way of the fruition of the word or, perhaps more accurately, the failure of those who hear it. We have seen, on the other hand, that the parable envisages the kingdom triumphing over all difficulties: the parable is optimistic, full of hope, but the commentary is more aware of the dangers and sounds a note of warning. However, it closes on an encouraging note, for the hearers standing on good ground hold the word fast. Once again Luke has an eye to his Gentile readers for the "noble and good" heart reflects the "beautiful and good", the moral ideal of the Greeks. These last hearers bring forth fruit "with endurance" or "in patience": their endurance contrasts with the fickleness and apostasy of the others.

The explanation of *The Sower* looks to the individual and is, indeed, a psychological study. Every man who has heard the gospel message is challenged to examine himself seriously and to weigh his reactions; for the word will find obstacles both outside of a man and within himself. And he who will boldly face up to these difficulties, the generous and virtuous man, he alone will be a disciple because he alone will bring forth the lasting fruit of the Christian life.

But has the interpretation wandered too far from the import of the parable? If the description of seed growing to the harvest depicts the irresistible development of the kingdom, how can it come to mean anything else? Yet we may reflect that the gospel of Jesus and the hearers of the gospel are the constituents of the kingdom. We may reflect, too, that the triumph of the kingdom is the triumph of the word of Jesus over the hearts of men. Therefore, if the explanation does go beyond the obvious meaning of the parable, it is still true to the ultimate meaning of the parable.

We may conclude that the interpretation of *The Sower*—at least in the form in which it has been transmitted—is a product of the primitive Church. However, the fact that all three synoptists have attributed it to Jesus is surely significant. It is reasonable to believe that he did sometimes explain his parables; this is suggested by Matt. 15, 15-20 and was, besides, the practice of the rabbis. We may hold, then, that the explanation now found in our gospels does go back to an interpretation by our Lord. Just as the first Christians and the evangelists commonly adapted and applied the parables of Jesus, here they have gone a stage further and have adapted his commentary on a parable. We have to be on our guard against a temptation to take a too restricted view of the scope of the tradition, and of the evangelists' role. The apostolic Church was passionately concerned with the teaching of Christ, but his words were living words, with an immediate and vital bearing on the Christian life.

THE MUSTARD SEED AND THE LEAVEN
Luke 13, 18-21; (Mark 4, 30-32; Matt. 13, 31-33)

18. And he said, "What is the kingdom of God like, and to what shall I compare it? 19. It is like a grain of mustard, which a man took and sowed in his own garden; and it grew and became a tree; and the birds of the sky lodged among its branches."
20. And again he said, "To what shall I compare the kingdom of God? 21. It is like leaven, which a woman took and hid in three measures of flour, until the whole was leavened."

We should recall that the phrase, "it is like a grain of mustard" means: it is the case with it (the kingdom) as with a grain of mustard seed.[4] In other words, it is not the seed itself but what happens to the seed that is significant, and the kingdom is really like the tree that grows out of the seed. The smallness of the mustard seed was proverbial—Mark describes it as "smaller than any of the seeds that are in the ground" (4, 31) —and yet, in favorable conditions, it could grow into a shrub some ten feet high. Indeed, Mark describes it as "the greatest of all shrubs" (verse 32) while Luke, like Matthew, uses "tree." All three evangelists specify that the birds come to nest in its branches. This is Old Testament imagery as may be seen from Daniel (4, 12) and Ezekiel (17, 22-23; 31, 6) where a tree sheltering the birds is a symbol for a great empire embracing all peoples. It may be that for Luke the birds signify the Gentiles.

Mark does not have *The Leaven* but in Matthew as well as in Luke it is a companion parable of *The Mustard Seed*. Here again the kingdom is not being compared to leaven but to what happens when leaven is placed in the mass of meal being prepared for baking; ultimately, the kingdom is like the leavened dough. It is noteworthy that in Romans 11, 16 St. Paul compares the whole people of God to a mass of dough.

In our modern and western manner we tend to read in *The Mustard Seed* and in *The Leaven* the story of the sure growth of the kingdom from its tiny beginning, the slow but steady permeation of human society by the leaven of the gospel. At least we are prone to stress this aspect primarily and almost exclusively. However, it appears that those who first heard the parables would have regarded them in a different light.

The modern man, passing through the tilled field, looks downwards and observes a biological development. The men of the Bible, walking over the same field, look upwards and see one miracle after another, a veritable awakening from the dead. It is thus that Jesus' hearers had understood *The Mustard Seed* and *The Leaven*, as parables of con-

trast: from the most insignificant beginnings, from out of apparent nothingness,
God was forming his kingdom.[5]

Both parables would have been the answer of
Jesus to an objection, latent or expressed: could
the kingdom really come from such inauspicious
beginnings? His reply is that the little cell of
disciples will indeed become a kingdom, and
the little lump of leaven will do its work.

Although, in these parables, the contrast between insignificant beginning and mighty achieve-
ment is primary, the idea of growth (the seed
grows into a plant) and of permeation (the leaven
does ferment the mass) is also present. Indeed,
the action of the leaven has a lesson of its own:
it is a hidden activity, but it is not quiet—it is
pervasive, resistless. Looked at in this way the
growth of the seed is also irresistible, it is a
miracle of God's action. For, in the last analysis,
if the kingdom does reach its full dimensions it
is not due to anything in the men who are the
seed of the kingdom; the growth is due solely to
the power of God (cf. 1 Cor. 3, 6-7). That is
why Jesus can speak with utter confidence of the
final stages of the kingdom. The finest comment
on these parables, bringing out this special aspect, is another parable given only by Mark, *The
Seed Growing Secretly*[6]:

It is with the kingdom of God as with a man
who has scattered seed upon the ground:
whether he sleeps or rises, night or day, the
seed sprouts and grows—he knows not how.
Of itself the earth produces first the blade,

then the ear, then the full grain in the ear. And when the grain is ripe, at once he puts in the sickle because the harvest has come (4, 26-29).

6

The Crisis

Jesus had come to found a kingdom that would spread out and embrace all men. Yet his own mission was limited to the Jewish people: "I have been sent only to the lost sheep of the house of Israel" (Matt. 15, 24); it was left to his disciples to teach all nations (28, 19). The coming of Christ marked a decisive moment in history; for the chosen people it was the moment of truth. In view of this moment they had been chosen, but they did not sense the urgency of it. They failed to recognize the challenge of the hour— that is their tragedy. And that is why Jesus insisted on opening their eyes. His solicitude and his anguish are manifest in the words addressed to Jerusalem:

> Jerusalem! Jerusalem! Thou who didst murder the prophets, and stone those who were sent to thee! How often would I have gathered thy children together, as a hen gathers her brood under her wings, but you would not have it so! (Luke 13, 34).

The great number of the parables of crisis bears striking testimony to the love and mercy of the Son of God even for those who sought his ruin. Truly, his prayer on the Cross: "Father, forgive them, for they know not what they do" (23, 34) is but the last echo of a life-long prayer.

THE CAPRICIOUS CHILDREN
Luke 7, 31-35; (Matt. 11, 16-19)

31. To what, therefore, shall I compare the men of this generation, and what are they like? 32. They are like children sitting in the market-place, shouting to one another and saying,
"We piped for you, and you did not dance; we wailed, and you did not weep."
33. For John the Baptizer has come neither eating bread nor drinking wine; and you say, "He has a demon!" 34. The Son of Man has come eating and drinking; and you say, "Look at him! a man who is a glutton and a wine-guzzler! a friend of publicans and sinners!" 35. Yet wisdom is justified by all her children.

Luke has set this little parable squarely in its context and the people addressed are named:

29. Now all the people, including the publicans, justified God when they heard him, and were baptized with John's baptism. 30. The Pharisees and doctors of the Law, however, spurned the intention of God to their own loss, in not being baptized by him. (7, 29-30).

Clearly, the attitude of the scribes and Pharisees is being criticized.

We can more accurately picture the little scene that Jesus describes if, with Matthew (11, 16) we accept that the children are "shouting to their playmates" and not "shouting to one another" (Luke 7, 32)—there is a difference! The children in question, *sitting* in the market place—the boys playing the flute and the girls chanting a funeral dirge—form part of a game. The remaining boys are expected to dance the wedding-dance (the round dance at weddings was performed by men) and the rest of the girls ought to have formed a funeral procession. Since they have failed to do so, the others loudly complain that they are spoil-sports.

The point of the parable, then, is the frivolous captiousness of these children and its accusation is obvious: the conduct of the scribes and Pharisees is no better. At this moment of crisis, when the last messengers of God had appeared, they hearkened neither to the preaching of repentance nor to the preaching of the good news but criticized and sulked.

The meaning of verse 35 seems to be that the children of Wisdom (God) in contrast to those who have remained obstinate, will recognize and accept the works of God.

THE RICH FOOL
Luke 12, 16-21

16. The land of a certain rich man produced abundant crops; 17. and he reflected with

himself, "What shall I do? for I have nowhere to store my crops. 18. This is what I
will do," said he; "I will pull down my store-
houses, and build larger ones; and there I
will store up my produce and my goods. 19.
Then I will say to my soul, O soul, thou hast
plenty of wealth laid up for many years:
take thine ease, eat, drink, be merry!" 20.
But God said to him, "Thou fool! this night
thy soul is required of thee; then whose
shall be the things with which thou hast pro-
vided thyself?" 21. So it is with one who
hoards wealth for himself and is not rich
toward God.

Though the parable begins at verse 16 it is
necessary to be aware of the immediate context
if we are to understand it or, rather, if we are to
see how the evangelist had understood it:

13. And one of the crowd said to him, "Master, bid my brother divide the inheritance
with me." 14. "Man," he answered him,
"who constituted me judge or arbiter over
you?" 15. Then he said to them, "Take
care and guard against all avarice; for one's
life does not consist in the abundance of
one's possessions." 16a. He then told them
a parable. (12, 13-16a).

The Jews were accustomed to submit similar
questions to their rabbis for a practical decision.
Here the man addresses Jesus as "Master" and
presents his case—it is a striking indication of
the standing Jesus had won with the people. He,
however, formally declines to have anything to
do in a matter of material possessions, he will

not seem to condone an attitude of absorption in this world's goods. With the phrase, "then he said to them," Luke links another saying which is, indeed, closely related to the foregoing incident for it warns against avarice and points out that riches will not guarantee a long life. Next, by means of another link-formula: "He then told them a parable" the evangelist fits in *The Rich Fool*. In this setting it illustrates the previous passage and serves as a warning against greed. No doubt it does this, but, as we shall see, when originally spoken by our Lord, it had a different bias.

The rich man is providing for the coming years when his crops may not be so abundant. He can then sit back and enjoy himself—the future is secure. "Soul" has the biblical meaning of the seat of the appetites, the seat of life; and at the very moment that his plans are laid God will take this life from him. Rightly is the man called "fool"—in Old Testament usage one who, in practice, denies God—for he had not only forgotten that his life was a loan which must be restored, but he had forgotten God, so absorbed had he become in his possessions. Verse 21 has all the appearance of a generalizing conclusion and is, in fact, omitted in some manuscripts; it serves to underline the fact that the man is indeed a "fool" and to emphasize the worthlessness of worldly possessions.

The climax of the parable is the man's confrontation by God in his moment of security. In his utter self-confidence he is quite unaware of the crisis that looms immediately before him. One thing at least is sure, Jesus did not speak this parable to illustrate the fact that death can come to a man at any time. Though it is not as obvious as most of the others, *The Rich Fool* finds its true place among the parables of crisis.

THE RICH MAN AND LAZARUS
Luke 16, 19-31

19. There was once a certain rich man, who was clothed in purple and fine linen, and daily lived in feasting and splendor. 20. And a certain beggar named Lazarus was laid at his gate covered with sores, 21. and longing to be fed with the scraps dropped from the rich man's table. Even the dogs came and licked his sores. 22. By and by, however, the beggar died, and was conveyed away by the angels into Abraham's bosom. The rich man also died and was buried; 23. and in the abode of the dead he raised his eyes, while in the midst of torment, and saw Abraham afar off, and Lazarus in his bosom. 24. Then shrieking out he cried, "Father Abraham, have pity on me, and sent Lazarus to dip the tip of his finger in water and cool my tongue; for I am tortured in this flame!" 25. "Child," replied Abraham, "remember that thou didst receive thy good things in thy lifetime, just as Lazarus received evils; so now he is consoled here, while thou art in anguish. 26. And besides all this, there is immovably fixed between us and you a vast abyss, so that those who wish to pass from us to you may not be able, and that none may cross over from you to us."

27. "Then I implore thee, Father," said he, "to send him to my father's house—28. for I have five brothers—to give them solemn warning, so that they too may not come into this place of torment." 29. "They have Moses and the Prophets," came the reply, "let them listen to them." 30. "Ah, no, Father Abraham!" was his answer; "but if some one goes to them from the dead they will repent." 31. "If they will not listen to Moses and the Prophets," came the reply, "neither would they believe were one to rise from the dead."

This striking story is not, of course, meant to be historical and no actual characters are in mind. The rich man was a worldling who did not look beyond the good things of life. In sharp contrast is the crippled beggar Lazarus; and though this poor creature lay daily at the rich man's gate the latter was unaware of his existence. It is sometimes suggested that the dogs show greater feeling and come to lick the beggar's sores. In fact they add to his misery: these are wild scavangers and the helpless Lazarus is unable to keep them at bay.

However great the contrast between the two men in this life it is far more pronounced in the after-life, though they have exchanged roles. In speaking to Jews, Jesus followed the prevalent notion of life beyond the grave. Throughout most of the Old Testament, *Sheol,* a dark, gloomy place, is the abode of all the dead, where good and bad lead a vague, unhappy existence. When eventually the doctrines of resurrection and of

retribution after death had evolved—not until
well into the 2nd century B.C.—this idea of
Sheol necessarily underwent a change. Then it
was thought to have two compartments: in one
the just quietly awaited the resurrection while
in the other the wicked were already being punished. Though these two sections were rigidly
separated (*cf.* verse 26) yet it was commonly
believed that both parties were in sight of each
other.

Death was described as "going to Abraham"
or, "being gathered to Abraham," an echo, or
modification of the frequent Old Testament
phrase, "gathered to the fathers," *i.e.,* to the pa-
triarchs. In our story Lazarus not only joins the
just but is given the place of honor at the right
hand of the patriarch. The phrase "to Abraham's
bosom" is clarified by John 13, 23—"One of his
disciples whom Jesus loved, was reclining upon
the bosom of Jesus," *i.e.,* at his right side and
leaning backward toward him.

The rich man also died and the manner of his
burial, in keeping with his wealth, merely em-
phasized the futility of his life, for he goes to the
place of torment. There he would wish for just
a single drop of the cool water that flowed
through the abode of the just and he begged his
father Abraham that Lazarus might be permitted
to render that simple service. Abraham does not
disown him: as a Jew he is, according to the
flesh, his son, but this is not enough to save him.

Verse 25 emphasizes the idea of the first part of
the parable. The reversal of roles is not a mere
mechanical process; verse 26 shows that the rich

man realized that his present state was a punishment, not simply a change of fortune, and
Lazarus was rewarded not for his poverty but for
his virtue. The abyss not only divides the two
compartments of *Sheol* but marks a definitive
separation between the two classes of dead. Is
it necessary to add that, in all this Jewish imagery,
we are not given anything remotely resembling
"a topography of hell"?

This is one of the two-pronged parables and,
true to form, the greater emphasis is on the second point, verses 27-31. But, just as in the first
part we are given no real description of hell so
here we can learn nothing of the psychology of
the damned. The reaction of the rich man is described from an ordinary human point of view:
his present sorry condition has at last opened his
eyes and he is understandably desirous that his
brothers should escape his fate.

Abraham answers that the five, who evidently
lead the same sort of life as their unhappy brother,
have "Moses and the Prophets" that is, the Old
Testament, and in it they can find perfectly clear-
cut teaching on their obligations to their less
fortunate brethren. The Law has provisions for
the poor (Ex. 22, 25; Deut. 24, 6, 10-13 ...),
Amos severely castigated thoughtless luxury and
forgetfulness of the poor (6, 4-7 8, 4) and a text of
Isaiah meets exactly the situation of Lazarus: what
God asks of his people, is "to share your bread with
the hungry, and bring the homeless poor into your
house; when you see the naked to cover him"
(58, 7).

The rich man makes one more plea: surely if

Lazarus were to come back from the dead his brothers would at last be warned and repent! The answer, however, is the same—a miracle, even a striking miracle, will not help those who have not made use of the means God has placed at their disposal; for a miracle will more readily convince one who is docile, one who is already disposed to accept the goodness and power of God. In John 5, 46-47 we find a close parallel: "If you believed Moses you would believe me, for he wrote about me. But if you do not believe his writings how are you to believe my statements?" The burden of the second part of the parable might be put like this: "If a man (says Jesus) cannot be humane with the Old Testament in his hand and Lazarus on his doorstep, nothing—neither a visitant from the other world nor a revelation of the horrors of Hell—will teach him otherwise."[1]

To whom was the parable addressed? There seems little doubt that, once again, it was aimed at the Pharisees. Elsewhere Jesus had refused explicitly to grant a like request: "This generation is a wicked generation; it demands a sign, yet no sign shall be given it but the sign of Jonah. For as Jonah became a sign to the Ninevites, so shall the Son of Man also be a sign to this generation" (11, 29-30). Jonah had pointed out the way of repentance and salvation, and so had Jesus; but though the Ninevites of the story had heeded the warning of the prophet the contemporaries of Jesus had not accepted him. They would receive no other sign because, like the five brothers of the parable, it would leave them un-

moved and unconvinced. As it is, they stand,
unheeding, before a crisis.

It is evident, however, that Luke has taken
the parable as addressed to the disciples; in fact
it is framed by the repeated phrase: "He also said
to his disciples" (16, 1; 17, 1). He sees it as a
warning about the danger of riches (it is that, of
course), a constant theme of his gospel. The
rich man is one who, thanks to his wealth, is
immersed in worldly pleasures and is forgetful
of God; all that his wealth has done for him is
to make him selfish and irreligious. Lazarus, on
the other hand, is in no such danger; obviously,
we must not regard him only as materially poor,
he is also "poor" in the religious sense of a virtuous, pious man (*cf.* 6, 20). In short, we are
shown the great danger of riches and we are
taught that poverty need not be an obstacle and
can be a help, to eternal happiness.

PLACES AT TABLE
Luke 14, 7-11

7. Then, observing how the invited guests
were choosing the first places at table, he
gave them a lesson (lit. he told a parable),
saying to them: 8. "When thou art invited
by any one to a wedding-feast, do not recline in the place of honor, lest one more
distinguished than thou be invited by him,
9. and the one who invited thee and him
come and say to thee, 'Give place to this
gentleman' and then thou begin with shame
to take the last place. 10. On the contrary,
when thou art invited, go and recline in the

last place; so that, when thy host comes, he may say to thee, 'My friend, go up higher!' Thou wilt then be honored in the presence of all thy fellow-guests. 11. For every one who exalts himself shall be humiliated; but he who humbles himself shall be exalted."

This parable, like *The Great Feast* (14, 15-24), is spoken in the course of a meal: Jesus was dining in the house of a Pharisee (14, 1). At first sight the passage seems to be a lesson in etiquette. Luke, however, calls it a "parable" and though, absolutely speaking, the underlying term *mashal* is wide enough to include a practical rule of conduct, he undoubtedly means something more than this. It is, of course, true that the situation is one which, at least in regard to the conduct of the guests, has arisen in fact and, later on, the scribes are characterized as those who "love places of honor at banquets" (20, 46). But what is in question is that such conduct, presented in parabolic guise, is censured and made the object of a warning.

The key to the passage is verse 11. This saying also occurs at 18, 14—as a generalizing conclusion to *The Pharisee and the Publican;* here, however, is its proper place. Our judgment is confirmed by the following passage: the advice to invite the poor rather than those who can make return (14, 12-13) ends with the words: "for thou shalt be repaid at the resurrection of the just" (verse 14b). In verse 11 the passive stands for the action of God and the future tense refers to the Judgment: "For every one who exalts himself will God humble, and he who humbles himself will God exalt." We are taken beyond the perspective of mere human relations and assured that God is no respecter of persons.

Now the drift of the parable is clear. If the Pharisees and scribes arrogated to themselves privileges and demanded preferential treatment, they did so on the grounds of their observance of the Law, on their standing as religious men. They took for granted that God would see things in that way, too, and render them the same preferential treatment, the first places in the kingdom —*The Pharisee and the Publican* admirably illustrates their outlook. Here they are quietly warned that they may be fortunate to get the lowest places. Besides, this, the decisive hour, is no time for details of precedence—if, indeed, there is any time at which precedence does matter! In a more general way, of course, the parable teaches the lesson of humility, a lesson valid for all and for all time. But as Jesus spoke it, the warning was more specific and pointed; it was one more attempt to move and to win these proud men.

THE POUNDS
Luke 19, 11-27; (Matt. 25, 14-30)

11. As they listened to all this, he related in addition a parable, because he was near Jerusalem and they supposed that the kingdom of God would immediately make its appearance.

12. "A nobleman," he accordingly said, "traveled to a distant country to receive a kingdom for himself, and to return. 13. And

calling ten of his servants he gave them ten gold-pieces, and said to them, 'Trade with these until I come.' 14. (Now his country-men hated him; so they sent an embassy after him with the petition, 'We are not will-ing that this person should reign over us.') 15. On his return, after having obtained the kingdom, he ordered those servants to whom he had given the money to be summoned, in order that he might ascertain how much each had made in his business transactions. 16. So the first appeared, saying, 'My lord, thy gold-piece has made ten gold-pieces more.' 17. 'Well done, good servant!' he said to him; 'because thou hast been faithful with a very little, thou shalt have the gov-ernment of ten cities.' 18. Then the second came, saying, 'My lord, thy gold-piece has made five gold-pieces.' 19. And to him also he said, 'And thou shalt be governor of five cities.' 20. Another also came, saying, 'Here, my lord, is thy gold-piece, which I have kept laid away in a napkin; 21. for I was afraid of thee, because thou art a hard man; thou takest up what thou didst not deposit, and thou reapest what thou didst not sow.' 22. He said to him, 'Out of thine own mouth will I condemn thee, thou wicked slave. Thou knewest me to be a hard man, taking up what I did not deposit, and reaping what I did not sow. 23. Why, then, didst thou not put my money in the bank, so that on my return I could have exacted it with interest? 24. Take the gold-piece from him,' he said to the attendants, 'and give it to the one who has the ten gold-pieces.' 25. 'Lord,' they said to him, 'he has ten gold-pieces!' 26. So, I tell you, that to every one who possesses shall be given; but from him who possesses not, even what he has shall be taken away from him. 27. (But as for those enemies of mine who did not wish me to reign over them, bring them here, and execute them in my presence)."

It cannot be doubted that *The Pounds* is a parallel to Matthew's parable of *The Talents*: these are two versions of the same parable. Yet, this confident assertion may appear unwarranted, seeing that the differences between them are so evident. Matthew's businessman becomes in Luke a nobleman who went abroad in order to make sure of his right to a throne (verse 12). Though an embassy of his own people tried to forestall him (verse 14) he did return as king; he set about rewarding his friends (verses 17, 19) and had his enemies put to death before his eyes (verse 27). These features are, admittedly, foreign to *The Talents* and, assembled together, they form the backbone of an originally independent parable, which we might name *The Pretender*.

The details recall an episode of 4 B.C. when, on the death of Herod the Great, his son Archelaus went to Rome to be confirmed in his possession of Judea. A deputation of Jews attempted to block his claim but Archelaus won out and, on his return, took a bloody revenge on those who had opposed him. This parable would have been a warning to the Jews, a parable of judgment (*cf.* Matt 10, 28, 32-33).

If we ignore verses 14 and 27 and reduce the nobleman of verse 12 to the status of a merchant as in Matthew, it is evident that we are left with a parable differing only in detail from Matt. 25, 14-30. It seems certain that the fusion of *The Pounds* and *The Pretender* was not made by Luke but had been brought about in the earlier tradition. It was very cleverly done but in verse 24f. the seam, not noticeable elsewhere, may be seen: the gold-piece or pound (*i.e., mina* = about $17.00) was taken from the unprofitable servant and given to a man who had just been made governor of ten towns!

The fact remains that the evangelist, finding the parables already combined, treated the whole as a single parable. And he has told us how he had understood this new parable for, by placing it in the context of the entry into Jerusalem (19, 11) he related it to the Parousia, the second coming of Christ. In Luke's eyes, the return of the king and the reckoning with his servants signified the return of Christ in glory.

Though this interpretation is firmly based on the teaching of Jesus who declared himself to be the Son of Man, King and Judge, it does not necessarily indicate the purpose of the original parables as Jesus had spoken them. We have remarked that *The Pretender* would have had in mind God's judgment on the Jews. What of *The Pounds?*

A nobleman entrusted a small sum of money to each of ten servants, bidding them trade with it while he was away. On his return he called them to account. Two of them had a nice profit

to show and were rewarded. Then another came
—Luke is not going to go through the whole ten
—who had kept the money laid away in a napkin, thereby showing remarkable carelessness;
for he should, at least, have taken the elementary
precaution of burying the money (*cf.* Matt. 25,
18).[2] He tries to brazen it out, but he is condemned out of his own mouth. The parable ends
at verse 24 because the present conclusion (verse
26) is an isolated saying of Christ added to widen
the application of the parable; it is also found
in Mark 4, 25; Matt 13, 12; Luke 8, 18.

We surely should notice that the center of interest is the conduct of the unprofitable servant
and his sentence—the others are foils to him.
According to the analogy of so many other parables, we should ask ourselves whether this man
is representative of any group in Israel. And we
have seen[3] that, in fact, our Lord had the scribes
in mind, and the parable was originally addressed
to them. They had not traded with the treasure
that God had given them but had kept it for
themselves: "Therefore, I tell you, the kingdom
of God shall be taken away from you and given
to a nation producing its fruits" (Matt. 21, 43).

We still have to take into account the parable
as it is presented by St. Luke. Since he passes it
on as he had found it in his source, we also learn
how the early Christians had understood it. The
parable has become an allegory or, at least, it has
taken on marked allegorical traits. The nobleman is Christ who had to leave this world before
returning in power and glory; his own citizens
who do not accept him are the Jews; the servants

are the disciples whom he expects to work with the "capital" he has given them. When he comes as Judge there will be a reckoning and the servants will be rewarded according to their deserts; the unbelieving Jews will receive particularly severe punishment. This last point is, of course, the lesson of *The Pretender* and the warning that the disciples must labor diligently and make full use of the charge they have received is implicit in *The Pounds*. The apostolic Church has been true, as always, to the teaching of its Master.

THE SERVANT: FAITHFUL OR UNFAITHFUL
Luke 12, 41-48; (Matt. 24, 45-50)

41. Peter then said, "Lord, art thou addressing this parable to us, or to all as well?" 42. And the Lord replied: "Who, now, is the faithful and prudent servant, whom his master will place over his domestics to give them their allowance of food at the proper time? 43. Happy is that servant, whose master on his arrival finds him thus engaged! 44. I tell you truly that he will place him over all his possessions. 45. But if that servant says in his heart, 'My master delays his coming,' and begins to beat the men servants and the maids, and to eat and drink and become drunk, 46. the master of that servant will come on a day when he is not expecting him, and at a moment which he is not aware of, and will severely scourge him, and assign him his place with the faithless.

47. And that servant who knew his mas-

ter's will, and did not prepare for him, nor act in accordance with his will, shall be flogged with many stripes; 48. but the one who knew not, yet did what deserved blows, shall be flogged with few. And of every one to whom much has been given much will be required; and of him to whom they have entrusted much, they will demand the more."

The question of verse 41 is absent from the parallel text of Matthew and its style betrays the hand of Luke; it refers to the preceding parable of *The Waiting Servants* (12, 36-38). The parable we are considering deals with the alternative conduct of a servant whom his master would place in charge of his affairs while he himself was absent on a long journey. If he were to prove faithful he would be richly rewarded but if he abused his authority he would be severely punished when the master had come and taken him by surprise. At the close of verse 46 the parable has been allegorized: it is no longer an earthly master who stands there, but the Son of Man who has come as Judge. The following verses are not in Matthew and have been added here by Luke; for the moment we shall leave them out of consideration.

It is sufficiently clear that the parable has been re-applied. As Jesus spoke it, the servant set in authority represented Israel's leaders and perhaps, more specifically, the scribes. "The scribes and Pharisees sit in Moses' seat" (Matt. 23, 2), they are the religious leaders of the people—but they had betrayed their trust. A scathing condemnation of this betrayal is given in Luke 11, 46-52—it is the best commentary on the parable. The early Christians, however, interpreted it as a warning to the Church's leaders; a perfectly natural extension of its meaning. The new interpretation is neatly brought out by Peter's question.

Verses 47-48a have no more than a loose link with the foregoing parable; they introduce the fresh idea that the punishment of disobedience will be in proportion to the knowledge of the master's will. Though Luke still refers the saying to the disciples it is almost certain that, originally, it would have contrasted the scribes' culpable rejection of Christ (they were the professional "searchers" of the Scriptures that spoke of him, *cf.* John 5, 39) with the far less culpable rejection of the ordinary people "ignorant of the Law" (7, 49).

Verse 48b is to be interpreted on its own. The passive and the impersonal forms stand for the divine name, and the verse might be rendered: "Of every one to whom God has given much will he require much; and of him to whom he has entrusted much will he demand the more." The saying may very well have been addressed to the religious leaders of Israel but it can, quite naturally, be applied to the leaders of the new Israel.

THE UNJUST STEWARD
Luke 16, 1-8[4]

1. There was a rich man who had a steward and he received complaints that this man was squandering his goods. 2. So he

summoned him and said: "What is this I hear of you? Produce the accounts of your stewardship, for you can no longer manage my affairs." 3. The steward thought to himself: "What am I going to do now that my master is taking the stewardship away from me? I am not strong enough to dig and too proud to beg. 4. Ah, I know what I must do so that when I have lost my position people will welcome me into their houses." 5. So he sent for his master's debtors one by one. He said to the first: "How much do you owe my master?" 6. He replied: "A hundred measures of oil." The steward said to him: "Take your bill, and sit down quickly and write fifty." 7. Then he said to another: "And how much do you owe?" He replied: "A hundred measures of wheat." The steward said to him: "Take your bill, and write in eighty."

8. And the Lord commended the dishonest steward for acting so astutely. For the children of this world are more astute in their dealings with their own kind than the children of light.

9. And I say to you, make friends for yourselves by means of unjust mammon, so that when it comes to an end, you may be received into the eternal habitations. 10. He who is faithful in a very little is faithful also in much, and the man who is dishonest in very little is dishonest also in much. 11. If, then, you have not proved trustworthy with the unrighteous mammon, who will trust you with the true riches? 12. And if you have not proved trustworthy with that

which is another's, who will give you what
is your own? 13. No servant can serve two
masters: for either he will hate one and love
the other, or he will be devoted to one and
despise the other. You cannot serve God
and mammon.

The first problem that presents itself is to determine the limit of the parable, and this depends
on the precise meaning of the words *kyrios*
("lord", "master") in verse 8. The steward's master may be meant and the verse is part of the parable. In that case verse 9 states the moral of the parable: as the action of the unjust steward was in
order that the debtors "may receive him into their
houses" so must the disciples of Jesus use the unrighteous mammon that they "may be received
into eternal dwellings."

However, it is preferable to take *kyrios* as
meaning "Lord" and so as referring to Jesus.[5]
If this be so, the parable ends at verse 7 and describes a rascal who, suddenly faced with a crisis
which may mean utter ruin, finds a drastic means
of coping with the situation. The method he
adopts in order to ensure his future security,
though quite unscrupulous, is manifestly resource-
ful.

In verse 8a we have the application of the parable by Jesus: "And the Lord commended the
unjust steward for his resolute action." The re-
mainder of the verse explains this unexpected
commendation: it is restricted to the cleverness
of worldly men in their dealings with one another.
Like the unjust steward, the hearers of the parable
stand before a crisis—they must act resolutely

or perish. It is significant that in verse 14 St. Luke numbers Pharisees among the audience and it is especially to such as they that the parable was addressed. In the person of Jesus the Kingdom of God has come among them; it is the decisive moment and, in effect, they are being urged to take the bold step of accepting him before it is too late.

But as the gospel stands, the parable is addressed to the disciples (16, 1) for so it was understood by the early Church. Yet, despite the change of audience, the point and message of it remain the same. For if Jesus could wish that Pharisees would recognize the hour of grace, he must surely also wish that his disciples would show as much resourcefulness in God's business as men of the world do in their own affairs. Still, the parable is difficult and the verses appended to it in Luke (9-13) show how the early Christian teachers wrestled with it. Indeed, this parable affords us a remarkable glimpse of the formative phase of the gospel tradition, a backstage view of the primitive Church in action.

The passage, verses 9-13, has been added to the parable by the familiar technique of catchwords. These are "unjust mammon" in verses 9 and 11 and "mammon" in verse 13, while the verses 9-11 are further linked by the repetition of *adikos* ("unjust," "dishonest"). In verse 8 we have seen the original application of the parable; now we find that verse 9 gives a different application. The meaning of the verse seems to be: "Do good works with the unjust mammon, that when it passes away, God may receive you into eternal dwellings."[6] The saying has been added here through verbal association: the reception into eternal habitations echoes the steward's wish— "so that people may receive me into their houses" (verse 4). It may have been originally addressed to tax-collectors or others classed as dishonest persons (trafficking in "unjust mammon"). But when it is attached to the parable as a secondary conclusion it points to a new interpretation of the parable. Now the steward is commended not for his resolution but for his wise use of money and the lesson for Christians is clear: they are to use the goods of this world in view of eternal life—almsgiving is evidently in mind.

There still remains the fact that the action of the steward is obviously unscrupulous — how then can he be in any sense an example? This difficulty was met by the addition of verses 10-13. Verse 10 states a general principle of conduct dealing with honesty or dishonesty in unimportant matters. In the next two verses the principle is applied to mammon and to everlasting riches. Since these verses are an example of perfect synonymous parallelism[7] it is clear that the "other riches" and "your own" of verse 12 mean respectively, the material wealth that must remain external to a man and the true spiritual riches which are his very own. The problem of the steward's conduct is solved: he is no longer an example but a warning. He has shown himself dishonest in very little, in the goods of this world; he may find shelter under the roofs of his equally unscrupulous friends, but he has no place in the eternal dwellings.

It would seem inevitable that the series should have been rounded off by the saying of verse 13. This occurs in an entirely different context in Matthew 6, 24 and is obviously a well-remembered saying of our Lord, one that made an immediate appeal to his disciples, for it epitomizes the obligations and the unending struggle of the Christian life.

Once we have realized that the parable proper ends at verse 7 and that its interpretation is indicated by our Lord's observation in verse 8 the passage is no longer the riddle that it must be otherwise. Verses 9-13 are isolated sayings, joined by catch-words, and together they form an elaborate secondary ending to the parable. It is noteworthy that these additions leave the substance of the parable unchanged—and the same is true elsewhere—but they do bear witness to a re-interpretation of a parable which is now applied by the primitive Church to the Christian community. It is, however, an application that is very much in accord with the parable as our Lord spoke it.

The resolute action which he recommends does embrace the generosity of verse 9, the faithfulness of verses 10-11 and the rejection of mammon in verse 13. The early Christians did not miss the point of the parable but, in applying it to themselves, they necessarily caused a shift of emphasis. They were able to bring to bear on their daily lives teaching that bore on the urgency of a great decision because their day to day lives were lived in the atmosphere of that decision: they had accepted the kingdom.

THE BARREN FIG TREE
Luke 13, 6-9

6. He related this parable: "A certain man had a fig tree planted in his vineyard; and he came looking for fruit on it, and found none. 7. So he said to the vine-dresser, 'See here! for three years I have come looking for fruit on this fig tree, and have found none. Cut it down; why should it still encumber the ground?' 8. But he answered him, 'Let it alone, sir, for this year too, until I dig about it and manure it. 9. It may perhaps bear fruit after that; but if not, thou shalt cut it down.' "

The planting of fig trees among vines is still not uncommon in Palestine. This tree had come to fruit-bearing age some three years before and since it gave every sign of remaining absolutely unfruitful the owner of the vineyard, understandably, felt that it should be cut down. The vine-dresser, however, pleaded for time; he would make a last supreme effort to save it—the putting on of manure was an unusual step.

The fig tree symbolizes Israel (*cf.* Hos. 9, 10; Jer. 8, 13) and, as in Jeremiah, a sterile and unfruitful Israel. Now the ax is laid to the root of the tree (Matt. 3, 10), this is the last chance. The time for repentance is short, desperately short. God's justice is tempered by his mercy, but his justice must be satisfied. If, in the short moment left, Israel does not bring forth the fruits of repentance, the time of grace will have run out; the most loving patience must have an end.

Throughout, the urgency of the hour is stressed and the warning is plain.

THE WICKED VINEDRESSERS

Luke 20, 9-16; (Mark 12, 1-12; Matt. 21, 33-46)

9. He also began to relate this parable to the people: "A man planted a vineyard, and let it out to vine-dressers, and went abroad for a long time. 10. And at the proper season he sent a servant to the vine-dressers, so that they might give him his share of the fruit of the vineyard. But the vine-dressers beat him, and sent him off with nothing. 11. And he sent still another servant; but they beat him also, treated him with indignity, and sent him off with nothing. 12. And he sent still a third; and this one they wounded, and flung him out. 13. Then the owner of the vineyard said, 'What shall I do? I will send my beloved son; perhaps they will reverence him.' 14. The vine-dressers, however, on seeing him reasoned among themselves, 'This is the heir; let us kill him, in order that the inheritance may be ours.' 15. Accordingly, they flung him outside the vineyard and murdered him. What therefore will the owner of the vineyard do to them? 16. He will come and bring destruction upon these vine-dressers, and will give the vineyard to others." On hearing this they said. "God forbid!"

All three synoptists have given this parable and a comparison of the three versions is instructive. It emerges, for instance, that originally the narrative must have described the sending of three successive servants as in Luke. In Mark 12, 5 the third is followed by "many others." Matthew 21, 34-36 has two groups of servants who are maltreated or killed. On the other hand, in Mark 12, 8, the son is murdered in the vineyard and his body is cast out of it; in Matthew 21, 39 and Luke 20, 15 he is killed outside the vineyard. These differences in detail—deliberate changes in fact—indicate the allegorizing tendency of the early Christians. We shall see, however, that these touches merely give greater relief to a factor which was present from the beginning.

Perhaps already at the opening words, and certainly as the parable progressed, its first hearers must have recalled, spontaneously, the familiar passage of Isaiah 5, 1-7: "My beloved had a vineyard on a very fertile hill . . . the vineyard of the Lord of hosts is the house of Israel . . . and he looked for justice, but behold, bloodshed." From the start, then, this vineyard is Israel and the vine-dressers are the leaders of Israel. The servants do represent the long line of prophets sent by God to his people; it is natural that later versions of the parable should have heightened the symbolism by touches such as those we have noted in Matthew and Luke.

Finally, there is the sending of the only son ("beloved son" = only son *i.e.,* the sole object of his father's affection) who is slain by these wicked men. Again, Matthew and Luke, by having the son murdered outside the vineyard, underline the identification of the son with Jesus, who died outside the walls of Jerusalem (John 19, 17;

Heb. 13, 12). The result of such conduct is that the vine-dressers will be punished and the vineyard given to others; the horrified "God forbid!" of the hearers (Luke 20, 16) indicates that they had indeed seen the point of the parable. Jesus had put before them a picture of Israel's history and had warned them that unless they speedily repented they would see God's vineyard pass from their hands forever. Even though Luke (verse 9) does say that the parable was addressed to "the people," Mark 11, 27; 12, 12 explicitly presents it as Christ's final warning to the Sanhedrin.

The passage is not pure allegory because, indeed, the story might have been drawn from life. Like 19th-century Ireland, Palestine in the 1st century was plagued by absentee landlordism and the owner's servants would have been no more welcome than the landlord's agents. The seemingly futile murder of the owner's son can be explained too, for the murderers conclude that the original owner has died and that his heir has come to claim his property. If they get rid of him the vineyard will have no claimant and they will remain in possession. But, as we have seen, the Jewish leaders did look behind the story to the Owner and Vineyard and Servants of their own religious history. What was more disturbing, they recognized Jesus' claim to be Son and they saw that they had been cast as the Wicked Vine-dressers. It is not surprising that "the scribes and the chief priests wished to lay hands on him at that very moment for they knew that he had told this parable against them" (Luke 20, 19; cf. Mark 12, 12; Matt. 21, 45-46).

Our treatment must have made clear that we regard the original parable as ending at 20, 16 (and, correspondingly, at Mark 12, 9 and Matt. 21, 41). The three evangelists conclude by quoting Ps. 117, 22 (Mark and Matthew also give verse 23 of the psalm): "A stone which the builders rejected, that one was made the cornerstone." It is obvious that this has nothing to do with the vineyard and it does not really fit the meaning of the parable. We begin to see the reason for the presence of the psalm-text at this point when we realize that in the early Christian preaching it was regularly applied to the resurrection of Christ (*cf.* Acts 4, 11; 1, Pet. 2, 4-7). In the parable, however, Jesus was accusing the Sanhedrites of plotting his death; there was no reference to the resurrection. The psalm-text was not part of the original parable but the reason for its insertion is manifest: "the early Church could never speak of the death of Jesus without proclaiming his resurrection."[8]

Luke alone includes the comment of verse 18: "Every one who falls upon that stone shall be broken to pieces; but upon whomsoever it shall fall, it shall grind him to dust." Many manuscripts do add the verse in Matthew (verse 44), but it is borrowed from Luke. The statement has in mind two Old Testament images. In Isa. 8, 14 Yahweh will become for Israel "a stone of offense and a rock of stumbling." In Dan. 2, 34f, 44f the kingdom of God is a "stone cut from a mountain by no human hand" which will break into pieces all world empires. The evangelist sees in Jesus the fulfillment of these messianic texts:

those who collide with him, like the unbelieving Jews, will be broken and when he comes again, as the great Judge, he will "grind them to dust." From first to last, it is a grim warning.

THE BUDDING FIG TREE
Luke 21, 29-31 (Mark 13, 28-31; Matt. 24, 34-35)

29. And he gave them an illustration: "Observe the fig tree, and all the trees. 30. When they are now budding forth, you see them and know of your own selves that summer is near. 31. So you also, when you see these events coming to pass, know that the kingdom of God is near."

In 21, 8-24 Luke gives Christ's prophecy of the destruction of Jerusalem in 70 A.D. The evangelist regarded this event as bringing definitively to a close the "times of Israel" and as marking the beginning of the "times of the nations" (verse 24); the latter is also the era of the Church. Though in verses 25-28 and again in verses 34-36 he looks beyond this event to the Second Coming, the parable of *The Fig Tree* (verses 29-31) still refers to the fate of Jerusalem.

Luke has followed Mark closely. If, in verse 29, he extended the image to "all the trees" this is due to his care to give a universal turn to what is specifically Palestinian; the fig tree is a notable herald of summer because, unlike the olive, for instance, it sheds its leaves and thereby awakens to new life. Similarly, the foregoing signs (verses 8-24) will herald the coming of the kingdom of God. What is meant is not its first coming—the

kingdom is already present in Christ himself—but
the second stage, of development and expansion,
the "times of the Church." This stage follows on
the catastrophe of 70 A.D. for that event, the end
of Jerusalem and the Temple, marked the decisive close of the Old Law. The many warnings
have gone unheeded and Israel will be swept
away.

THE CLOSED DOOR

Luke 13, 22-30
(Matt. 7, 13-14; 25, 10-12; 7, 22-23; 8, 11-12)

22. He was traveling on through towns and
villages, teaching and making his journey
toward Jerusalem. 23. And some one asked
him, "Lord, are they few who are saved?"
24. But he said to them: "Strive to enter by
the narrow door; for many, I tell you, will
seek to enter it, and shall be unable. 25.
When once the master of the house has risen
and closed the door, and you begin, standing
outside, to knock at the door, saying, 'Lord,
open to us!' and he shall say to you in answer, 'I know not whence you are!' 26. then
you will begin to say, 'It is we who ate and
drank in thy company and thou didst teach
in our streets'; 27. and he will say, 'I tell
you, I know not whence you are! Begone
from me all you doers of iniquity.' 28. There
shall be weeping and the grinding of teeth,
when you see Abraham, Isaac and Jacob,
and all the prophets in the kingdom of God,
and you yourselves thrust out. 29. And they
shall come from east and west, and from
north and south, and shall recline in the

kingdom of God. 30. And behold, some are last who shall be first, and some are first who shall be last!"

In Part I we explained how, by different methods, the early Christians adapted and interpreted the parables of Jesus and in chapter V we examined the developed explanation of *The Sower*. Now, in the present passage, we come upon a case where a new parable has been composed of various sayings of our Lord, sayings that may be found isolated in Matthew. It is unlikely that the fusion is due to Luke; it is much more probable that the evangelist found the passage in his source and that he reproduced it much as he had found it.

The question of verse 23 was a contemporary one and the usual answer was that all Israel would have a place in the future kingdom; even the ordinary people, though "ignorant of the Law" (John 7, 49) would not be excluded—only tax-gatherers and similar types, "sinners," would be debarred. Though the question is concerned with the salvation of Israel only, it is still one that Jesus refused to answer directly. Instead, he warned his questioners that an effort is demanded of them; it is no easy matter to lay hold of eternal life (*cf. Matt.* 7, 13-14). The second part of verse 24 is explained by the following verse. In verse 25 we are dealing no longer with a narrow door but with a closed door and the image is that of the Messianic Banquet. A comparison with Matt. 25, 10-12 indicates that the master here is Christ himself. The Jews had not accepted him, they had not entered into the Kingdom while they had the chance; now it is too late, the door is firmly closed. This explains, too, why those of verse 24 were unable to enter—they were too late.

While in Matt. 7, 22-23 the rejected ones are unworthy Christians here, in verses 26-27, they are still the Jews. It is not enough for them to have been contemporaries of Jesus, to have seen him, to have heard him, to have eaten with him; they had not accepted him and now they are cast off. Their chagrin will be all the greater when they see not only their own great ancestors, but the Gentiles too, present at the Banquet (verses 28-29). These same verses, in Matt. 8, 11-12, conclude the account of the cure of the centurion's servant. Finally, verse 30 is a familiar secondary conclusion (*cf.* Mark 10, 31; Matt. 20, 16) added here in view of the contrast between Gentiles and Jews (verses 28-29).

It is obvious that most of this passage is in the spirit of the parables of crisis and the sayings from verse 25 onward are a group of warnings to Israel. What is not so easy to see is why the sayings should have been built into a new parable since concern with the fate of the Jews was not a prevalent preoccupation of the early Church; indeed, we have seen time after time that the tendency was to give a wider interpretation to specifically Jewish parables. But the tension between Jews and Gentiles did exist and this passage reflects it. It is also, in its way, a commentary—in his own words—on our Lord's answer to the question of verse 23, an emphasizing of the warning implied in the "narrow door."

The unbelieving Jews had not found their way into the Kingdom. Their fate is a warning to all that a practical acceptance of Christ, a faith showing itself in action, is necessary for salvation. And so, rather incongruously—since our object is to get back to the original meaning of the parables of Jesus— we close this chapter with a parable which is not really his, even though it is composed entirely of his sayings. However, it has its place here for it marks a climax, the closing of a door. The parables of crisis had fallen on deaf ears.

7

God's Mercy for Sinners

The divine intervention in history that is the kingdom or reign of God was accomplished by the coming of the Son of God. It is the supreme manifestation of divine love: "The love of God was displayed in our own case by the fact that God has sent his only-begotten Son into the world, in order that we might live through him. The love lay in this—not that we loved God, but that he loved us, and sent his Son to be an expiation for our sins" (I John 4, 9-10).

Our Lord constantly strove to bring men to an awareness of the Father's great love for them. The parables of crisis face the problem at its most crucial point for the proud and self-righteous leaders of the people were loath to believe that God might be displeased with them and could not conceive that their world was on the verge of crashing about their ears. We shall see that they completely failed to understand or appreciate God's infinite concern for sinners.

That "the Son of Man came to seek and to save the lost" (Luke 19, 10) was a statement they could not understand and Jesus' practice of consorting with sinners was a scandal to them: "Look at him! a man who is a glutton and a wine-guzzler! a friend of publicans and sinners!" (7, 34). Time and again our Lord had to face the same charge and tirelessly he justified his conduct. He did this consistently because he was jealous of the honor of his Father, because he felt constrained to vindicate the excess of divine love. For the very same reason he himself sought out sinners; and also because he loved them as his Father loved them.

The *Sitz im Leben* of the parables of mercy dramatically underlines the infinite distance that separates God from man: God loves sinners with an infinite love yet man cannot be brought to tolerate his fellow-man. And it illustrates, too, the sublime courtesy of Christ who answered his carping critics not curtly but with patience, in words of quiet charm. But, most of all, these parables bring us hope, conscious as we are—unless we stand in the unhappy situation of the Pharisees—of our own sinfulness: our Savior proved the sincerity of his words, manifested his love for sinners, by dying on a Cross.

THE TWO DEBTORS
Luke 7, 41-43 (Context—Luke 7, 36-47)

36. One of the Pharisees having asked him to dine with him, he entered the Pharisee's house, and reclined at table. 37. And

behold, a woman who was a sinner in the city, on learning that he was at table in the Pharisee's house, brought an alabaster flask of perfumed oil, 38. and standing behind at his feet weeping, began to bathe his feet with her tears and wipe them with the hair of her head, while she kissed his feet, and anointed them with the perfume. 39. But the Pharisee who had invited him, on seeing this, said to himself, "If this man were a prophet, he would have recognized who and what kind of woman it is who is touching him; that, in fact, she is a sinner." 40. "Simon," said Jesus answering him, " I have something to say to thee." "Master," said he, "say on."

41. *"A certain money-lender had two debtors, one of whom owed him five hundred denarii, and the other fifty. 42. As they both had nothing with which to pay, he freely forgave them both. Which of them, now, would love him more?"* 43. *"I suppose,"* said Simon in reply, *"it would have been the one to whom he forgave more."* *"Thou hast judged rightly,"* he said to him.

44. Then, turning toward the woman, he said to Simon, "Dost thou observe this woman? I came into thy house; thou gavest me no water for my feet; but she has bathed my feet with her tears and wiped them with her hair. 45. Thou gavest me no kiss; but she, from the time I came in, has not ceased to kiss my feet. 46. Thou didst not anoint my head with oil; but she has anointed my feet with perfume. 47. For this, I tell thee, her sins, which are many, are forgiven, be-

cause she has loved much; but he to whom little is forgiven loves but little."

This little parable must be read and interpreted against the background of the narrative in which it is set. Perhaps nowhere else as in this wonderful passage, the story of "the woman of the city who was a sinner" do we see Christ as St. Luke saw him. The Lord does not hesitate between the self-righteous Pharisee and the repentant sinner, and his words are clear and to the point: "Her sins, her many sins, are forgiven her, for she has loved much" (7, 47); her action was an extraordinary display of gratitude for the mercy she had received.

In the parable, and throughout the narrative indeed, "love" means "thankful love," "gratitude." Jesus' question then is: "Which of them would be the more grateful?" And in the context Simon is told: This woman, despite her sins, is nearer to God than you for she has, what you lack, gratitude. At the same time, of course, the great goodness of God is manifest. The money-lender of the parable, who remits the debt simply because his creditors are unable to pay, is hardly typical of his calling; it is obvious that the parable portrays a God who is ready to forgive any debt. God is, Jesus says, so infinitely good and merciful. And, to add force to his words, the woman, shedding tears of gratitude, is a living parable of the divine mercy.

THE GREAT FEAST
Luke 14, 16-24   (Matt. 22, 1-10)

16. A man gave a great banquet and invited many people; 17. and he sent his servant at the time of the banquet to tell those who had been invited to come, for all was now ready. 18. But they all with one accord began to excuse themselves. The first told him, "I have bought some land, and am obliged to go out and see it; I beg thee have me excused." 19. Another said, "I have bought five yoke of oxen, and am going to try them; I beg thee have me excused." 20. And another said, "I have married a wife, and owing to this I am unable to come." 21. The servant accordingly came and reported all this to his master. Then the master of the house was angry, and said to the servant, "Go out right away into the streets and alleys of the city, and bring in here the poor and the maimed and the blind and the lame!" 22. The servant reported, "What you have ordered, sir, has been done, and there is yet room." 23. Then the master said to the servant, "Go out into the roads and along the hedges, and compel people to come in, so that my house may be filled! 24. For I tell you, that no one of those men that were invited shall taste of my banquet!"

Since the parable, and Matthew's version of it, have been treated at some length above[1] it is unnecessary to delay over it. We should, however, draw attention to the setting. Jesus was dining with "one of the princes of the Pharisees" (14, 1) and the parable was prompted by a remark of a fellow-guest: "Happy is he who shall feast in the kingdom of God" (14, 15)—a banquet was a well-known figure for messianic blessedness (*cf*. Isa. 25, 6) Because of this, and in view of *The Places at Table* (14, 7-11), it is a warning to the Pharisees: they may not be present at the messianic banquet, and so it points to the crisis (*cf*. verse 24). But, ultimately, it explains why "the poor and the maimed and the blind and the lame"—who stand for the tax-collectors and sinners, these classes despised by the Pharisees—have won their way into the kingdom. It is a parable of mercy.

The Pharisee and the Publican
Luke 18, 9-14

9. He told this parable also to some who were confident of their own righteousness, and despised all others: 10. "Two men went up to the temple to pray, the one a Pharisee, the other a publican. 11. The Pharisee stood and prayed thus about himself: 'O God, I thank thee that I am not like the rest of men—extortioners, unjust, adulterers—or even like this publican. 12. I fast twice in the week. I give tithes of all my income!' 13. But the publican, standing far off, would not so much as raise his eyes to heaven, but smote his breast, saying, 'O God, be merciful to me the sinner.' 14. This man, I tell you, went back to his house justified rather than the other. For every one who exalts

himself shall be humiliated; but he that humbles himself shall be exalted."

We are left without any doubt that this parable was spoken to Pharisees because the "some who were confident of their own righteousness and despised all others" can refer to no one else.

From the very first the parable is a dramatic contrast. The two men who at the same time pray in the Temple, represent the two extreme strata of Jewish society: the Pharisee, taking his stand on the minute observance of the Law, is the embodiment of Jewish faith and morality; the tax-collector is, by his office, one who does not observe the Law and scarcely merits the name of Jew. The Pharisee comes boldly into the presence of God. He is not necessarily ostentatious—indeed, he prays to himself (rather than "about himself")—and his posture is not an indication of pride since it was customary to pray standing; the tax-collector also stands. Nor is the Pharisee a hypocrite, for everything he says is true.

What is wrong with his prayer is not what he says but what he does not say. Jewish prayers begin by giving praise and glory to God but this man thanks God for what he himself is. Then he goes on to works of supererogation. The Law knew only one day of fast in the year—the Day of Atonement—but he fasts twice a week (every Monday and Thursday) and he does so for the sins of the people. Likewise his payment of tithes went far beyond the demands of the Law. He is quite convinced that he stands right with

God and he feels no need to ask forgiveness. This picture of the Pharisee is not an unjust one; an extant prayer of about the same period is a remarkably close parallel to the text of Luke:

> I thank thee, Yahweh, my God, that thou has given me my lot with those who sit in the house of learning, and not with those who sit at the street-corners. For I rise early and they rise early: I rise early to study the words of the Torah and they rise early to attend to things of no moment. I weary myself and they weary themselves: I weary myself and win a reward while they weary themselves to no profit. I run and they run: I run towards the life of the world to come and they run towards the pit of destruction.[2]

The tax-collector does not come boldly into the Temple but, conscious of his sins, stands at a distance from the Holy Place. But he does come into God's presence and his whole attitude, downcast eyes and the beating of his breast, betrays his feelings. Like the Pharisee he is thinking of himself, but what he contemplates is his sin and misery and he feels no temptation to compare himself with other men. His prayer is very simple, a cry from the heart, a cry for forgiveness.

The Pharisees who had listened to the parable up to this point would perhaps have expected to be told that God does not hear sinners (cf. John 9, 31). They might have been prepared to hear that God did grant pardon to the tax-collector— in virtue of the justice of the other. They were quite unprepared for the verdict of Jesus. The

tax-collector was justified—his sins were forgiven; he had asked for pardon and his prayer
was heard. The Pharisee was not justified,[3] his
sins were not forgiven—because he had not asked
for pardon. His error, his blindness, was that
he did not see himself for what he was. He, too,
was a sinner, he, too, had need to pray the prayer
of the tax-collector. Once again, Jesus tries to
open the eyes of these blind guides.

In view of the explicit address of the parable
to the Pharisees, verse 14b is obviously a generalizing conclusion; the saying is also found in 14,
11 and in Matt. 23, 12. This is, as we have seen,
the very simplest method of applying to the new
Christian situation a parable that had been spoken
by Jesus to his adversaries. And the parable has
indeed a message, and a warning, for every Christian. But, while recognizing the universal import of it, we must not lose sight of its first setting
in the ministry of our Lord, nor overlook the
stress it lays on the forgiving mercy of God.

The Parables of Mercy

In chapter 15 of his gospel St. Luke has
grouped three parables: *The Lost Sheep, The
Lost Coin* and *The Prodigal Son*. More than
that, he has explicitly established the original
Sitz im Leben of all three. At the beginning of
the chapter he tells us that the tax-collectors and
sinners were flocking to our Lord and listening
to him and that the Pharisees and scribes, who
regarded such people as outcasts,[4] were scandalized by these goings-on. "This man," they grum-

bled, "welcomes sinners and even eats with them."
What was our Lord's reaction? "He accordingly
told them this parable" (*i.e., The Lost Sheep*)
and followed it with the parable of *The Lost Coin*.
Immediately after the latter we read, "he also
said" (verse 11) and then comes *The Prodigal
Son*. In other words, the parables are a reply to
the charge of the Pharisees: Jesus defends his
conduct. He consorts with sinners precisely because he knows that God is a loving Father who
welcomes the repentant sinner. God does not
regard sinners as outcasts but follows them with
love and receives them tenderly when they come
back to him.

THE LOST SHEEP
Luke 15, 4-7 (Matt. 18, 12-14)

4. What man among you who has a hundred sheep, and loses one of them, will not
leave the ninety-nine in the desert, and go
in search of the lost one until he finds it?
5. And when he has found it he lays it on
his shoulders rejoicing; 6. and on coming
home he calls his friends and neighbors together, saying to them, "Congratulate me,
for I have found my sheep that was lost!"
7. So I tell you there will be more gladness
in heaven over one sinner who repents, than
over ninety-nine righteous persons who
need no repentance.

In the first of the three parables in answer to
the Pharisees' complaint Jesus tells of the
shepherd who went in search of the sheep that

was lost and of his joy when he had found it. The solicitude of the man is such that he leaves the ninety-nine in the desert, unattended, while he searches for the other. And his joy at finding the lost sheep is so great that he must tell his neighbors of it. The moral of the story is stated in emphatic terms: "Even so, I tell you, God will have more joy over one sinner who repents than over ninety-nine persons who need no repentance" (verse 7). This does not mean that God loves the sinner more than the just—any more than the shepherd had shown greater care for the sheep before it had strayed. The Last Judgment appears to be in question: God will rejoice that, together with the just, he can also welcome home the repentant sinner. Such is the goodness of God. And that is why Jesus, too, seeks out sinners. The Pharisees and scribes, by caviling at his conduct, are criticizing the divine goodness.

THE LOST COIN
Luke 15, 8-10

8. Or what woman, possessing ten silver coins, if she loses one coin will not light a lamp and sweep the house, and search carefully until she finds it? 9. And when she has found it, she calls her friends and neighbors together saying, "Congratulate me for I have found the coin which I had lost!" 10. So, I tell you, there is gladness in the presence of the angels of God over one sinner who repents.

This parable, proper to Luke, teaches the lesson of *The Lost Sheep* all over again; it is typical of the evangelist that he should have brought a woman into the picture. Since it has precisely the same moral as the other parable it will be enough to comment on a detail or two.

Ten drachmas ("silver coins") was a modest sum, but the loss of even one coin is of great concern to a woman in humble circumstances. She had to light a lamp because the poor, windowless house—the only opening being a low door—was in near darkness. The phrase "in the presence of the angels of God" (verse 10) is a doubly periphrastic rendering of the divine name: (1) the angels; (2) in the presence of God — the angels are those who stand "in the presence of" God. We are told that God is glad over one sinner who repents (*cf.* verse 7).

This and the previous parable consider the conversion of a sinner from God's point of view. God has sent his Son "to seek out and save what was lost" (19, 10) and Jesus' actual concern for sinners is the concrete proof that God does more than desire that sinners should repent.

THE PRODIGAL SON
Luke 15, 11-32

11. He also said: "A certain man had two sons, 12. and the younger of them said to his father, 'Father, give me the portion of the property which falls to my share,' So he divided the property between them. 13.

Not many days after, the younger son, having collected everything, traveled to a distant land, and there squandered his fortune in voluptuous living. 14. And when he had spent all, a terrible famine occurred in that country, and he himself began to be in want. 15. So he went and engaged himself to one of the citizens of that country, who sent him upon his farm to feed swine. 16. And he longed to fill his stomach with the carob-pods on which the swine fed; and no one gave him anything. 17. Coming then to himself he said, 'How many hired men in my father's service have bread enough and to spare, while I am perishing here with hunger! 18. I will rise and go to my father, and will say to him, Father, I have sinned against heaven and in thy sight; 19. I am no longer worthy to be called thy son; make me as one of thy hired men.' 20. So he rose and returned to his father. But while he was still a long way off, his father saw him, and was moved with pity; and running to meet him he fell upon his neck and kissed him. 21. 'Father,' said the son to him, 'I have sinned against heaven and in thy sight; I am no longer worthy to be called thy son.' 22. 'Be quick,' said the father to his slaves, 'and bring out the best garment, and clothe him in it; and put a ring on his finger, and sandals on his feet; 23. and fetch the calf that was fattened, and kill it; and let us feast and have a merry time. 24. For this son of mine was dead, and has come to life; he was lost, and is found!' And they accordingly began to be merry.

25. "Now his elder son was out on the
farm; and as he returned and drew near the
house, he heard music and dancing. 26. So
calling one of the servants he asked what
this meant. 27. 'Thy brother has come,' he
answered him, 'and thy father has killed the
fattened calf, because he has him back safe
and sound.' 28. He was indignant, however,
and refused to go in; so his father came out,
and implored him. 29. But in reply he said
to his father, 'Look here! I have been slaving
for thee so many years, and have never dis-
obeyed a command of thine; yet thou hast
never given me a kid, so that I might have
a merry time with my friends! 30. But as
soon, as this son of thine comes back, who
has squandered thy property upon harlots,
thou must kill for him the fattened calf!'
31. 'Son,' he answered him 'thou art always
with me, and all that is mine is thine. 32.
But it was right that we should be merry
and rejoice, because this brother of thine
was dead and has come to life; he was lost
and is found.' "

The most widely known and best-loved parable is, beyond doubt, *The Prodigal Son* —
though it might be better named, as we shall see,
The Loving Father; furthermore, its lesson appears to be quite obvious. It is possible, however, that we may have missed the point: we fix
our attention on the prodigal, but the parable
speaks of *two* sons—what has become of the
other? It may come as something of a surprise
to learn that our Lord meant the emphasis to
fall on the conduct of the elder son.

According to the Jewish law of the day, the share of the younger of two sons would be one-third of his father's property. The young man of the parable lost no time in turning his portion into cash and then cleared off to a distant country. There was nothing very extraordinary about this because, at the time, half a million Jews lived in Palestine and four million outside of it. However, unlike most of his countrymen, he soon ran through his fortune and found himself, in face of a famine, quite penniless, when, we may suppose, money could have gotten him something in the black market. He was quickly made to feel that, in the circumstances, nobody had any thought for an impoverished foreigner and the only job he could get was minding pigs. At once he saw that even the pigs were better treated than himself for they, at least, were given something to eat. This brought him to his senses and he realized that his father's servants were infinitely better off than he was in his present situation. He then and there determined to go back home, and already began to rehearse the plea that he would address to his father.

Meanwhile, the father had not forgotton his son and was looking forward to the day of his return. When at last he saw him coming he ran to meet him and greeted him tenderly. The son could get through only the opening part of his little speech, and his father scarcely heard even that much. He hastened to clothe the young man in fine garments and had a signet ring put on his finger: this was an indication of rank. Similarly, he was given shoes, for he was no barefoot servant but a son of the family. Then followed a joyous feast, with song and dance: "For this son of mine has come back to life; he was lost and is found."

This would appear to be the end of the parable and the message of it seems to be quite clear. It is obvious that the prodigal and the father thinly veil the sinner and his God. The sinner goes his unthinking way and is only brought up short when his world breaks in pieces about him. But a good God is looking for his return, waiting for the first sign of repentance, to welcome him back with infinite love. That is what God is like, our Lord tells us, so incredibly good. It is not at all the prodigal son who should hold our attention but the far more prodigal Father.

However, the parable is not ended, the elder son has his place in it. He, the sober, industrious type, had been about his work when the other arrived, and he knew nothing of his arrival until he heard the sounds of merrymaking. When he found out what the rejoicing was all about he sulked and refused to go in, and his father came to plead with him. Angrily, he broke into his father's entreaties: He had slaved all his life, had always done what he was told but nobody had ever thought of throwing a party for *him!* (How wonderfully true to life). And he concluded— in the splendid rendering of a modern version —[5] "But now that this son of yours turns up, after running through your money with his women, you kill the fatted calf for him!" His father gently pointed out that he need have no fear of being displaced, for he was the heir; but he really ought to enter into the spirit of the occasion and rejoice: "Your brother here was dead and has come back to life, was lost and is found." Notice how the second part ends with the very same words as the former and so the whole is welded into a unit; we may not just stop at the first half.

The younger son obviously stands for the sinner; who does his elder brother represent? We readily find the answer when we consider the context, for this parable, like the other two, is a reply to the charge of the Pharisees: Jesus defends his conduct. The elder son of the parable —stirred no doubt by jealousy—is offended by the generosity (which he regards as weakness) of his father; the Pharisees and scribes cavil at the goodness of God.

We surely cannot imagine that this awareness of the original application has blunted the message of the parable for us. *The Prodigal Son* does, indeed, bring vividly before us the loving mercy of a forgiving God. It teaches us that no sinner is utterly cast off, without hope; if he turns, in repentance, he will certainly be received and welcomed. But we are warned, too, that we must not be critical of the ways of God.

The parable teaches all this but it becomes more meaningful when we see it in its historical context, as spoken by the Savior, because then it tells us something of our Lord as well. He did not merely preach God's love for the sinner in words, he preached it in action by seeking out sinners. Then he pointed out to the Pharisees and scribes how very wrong their attitude was; but he did not condemn. With great condescension, pitying their blindness, he quietly defended himself, justified his conduct in the eyes of these self-righteous men—for they too, even if they did not know it, were prodigal children. And he, like his Father, is prodigal of love.

8

Disciples

Not all the parables warn of the imminence of the crisis, not all defend the conduct of Jesus or vindicate the honor of God. We have studied already some that tell of the growth and development of the kingdom; now, in conclusion, we turn to words of instruction for the subjects of the kingdom. These parables will teach us what a disciple should be like and what may be required of him.

The true disciple will heed and will realize what the call of Jesus may demand of him and then, resolutely, he will answer that call. His service will find expression in action, it cannot be a matter of words only. As he strives to serve his Master as faithfully as he can he will be aware that he never does more than may be expected of him. At all times he must be vigilant and never give way to self-confidence. But, he can be of good heart because he has a Father in heaven who will surely hear his prayers. And he must constantly bear in mind that what his Lord asks of him, more than anything else, is the unlimited practice of fraternal charity:

> By this all men shall know that you are my disciples, if you have love for one another (John 13, 35).

COUNTING THE COST
Luke 14, 28-33

28. Which of you, wishing to build a castle, will not first sit down and calculate the cost, to ascertain whether he has enough to complete it, 29. lest, having laid a foundation, and not being able to finish, all the beholders should begin to ridicule him, 30. saying, "This man began to build, and was unable to finish!" 31. Or what king, as he goes to encounter another king in war, will not first sit down and deliberate whether he is able with ten thousand men to meet the one who is advancing against him with twenty thousand. 32. And if he is not, he will, while the other is still at a distance, send an embassy to sue for conditions of peace. 33. So therefore not one of you can be my disciple who does not renounce all that he has.

Luke has set these two parables in the context of self-renunciation: "If anyone comes to me, and does not hate his father and mother and wife and children and brothers and sisters, yes, and his own life even, he cannot be my disciple" (14, 26). The exhortation is couched in its strongest terms ("hate" here means detachment) and the situation envisaged is the relatively rare one in

which a man is called upon to choose between
the following of Christ and his own relatives. The
twin parables drive home the lesson that disciple-
ship does involve commitment, it cannot be un-
dertaken thoughtlessly.

Although the parables appear to say the same
thing they are, in fact, complementary. In the
first, the builder is free to undertake his construction or not, he is considering the matter in the
abstract. The king, on the other hand, is already
up against it: his country has been invaded (the
other king is "advancing against him"), therefore
he must act. "In the first parable Jesus says, 'Sit
down and reckon whether you can afford to follow me.' In the second he says, 'Sit down and
reckon whether you can afford to refuse my demands.' "[1] For, indeed, these are the two factors
in the call to follow Christ: we have to count the
cost both of accepting that invitation and of re-
jecting it. He who comes to Christ must come
with his eyes wide open.

The parables may seem discouraging, but they
are to be understood in much the same way as
the saying of verse 26. The following of Christ
is at all times a serious business and, in certain
circumstances, it can be an even more serious
business. It is true, for instance, in time of persecution; it is scarcely less true in the modern world
where the Christian is called upon to renounce
so much that is taken for granted by others. If
he does come after his Master he must be prepared to take up his cross and carry it (verse 27)
while, at the same time he cannot, without sin,
fail to live up to his obligations as a Christian.

The encouraging thing is that the Christ who calls him knows the cost involved and knows, too, human frailty and will lavish his grace on the one who really tries to answer his call.

Verse 33 was probably added by St. Luke, in the light of verse 26f, and is a practical consequence of the two parables rather than their moral.

THE TWO BUILDERS
Luke 6, 47-49; (Matt. 7, 24-27)

47. Every one who comes to me, and listens to my words, and puts them into practice— I will show you to whom he is like. 48. He is like a man building a house, who dug, and kept deepening, and laid a foundation upon rock. And when a flood came, the torrent broke upon that house, and could not shake it; for it had been well built. 49. But he who listens and does not practice is like a man building a house upon the ground without a foundation; against which the torrent broke, and at once it fell; and the wreck of that house was utter.

24. Every one, therefore, who listens to these words of mine, and puts them in practice, shall be compared to a wise man who built his house upon the rock; 25. and the rain descended, and the floods came, and the winds blew, and beat upon that house, and it fell not, for it had been founded upon the rock. 26. And every one who listens to these words of mine, but does not put them into practice, shall be compared to a foolish man, who built his house upon the sand; 27.

and the rain descended, and the floods came, and the winds blew, and dashed against that house, and it fell; and utter was its ruin!

Like Matthew, Luke has this parable at the close of the Sermon on the Mount; we have given the texts of both versions because it is instructive to compare them. Luke's treatment is a perfect example of how an evangelist may vary details to suit his own general purpose.

In Matthew the contrast is between a house built on rock and one built on sand and the causes of destruction are heavy rain, which brings torrents of water beating against the house, and a violent wind. These conditions are typically Palestinian: the heavy winter rains are always accompanied by a gale and often by thunder and lightning. As a result, floods of water rush along the *wadi*-beds (a *wadi* is a water-course which is dry except after heavy rain); the "sand" on which the house was built is the floor of such a *wadi* and the man who built there was asking for trouble.

Luke has proceeded to change the details so that the parable might be more readily intelligible to his non-Palestinian readers. He is not concerned with the position of the house but describes whether or not it was given a sound foundation—the wise man "dug deep." The flooding is not caused by torrential rain but by an overflowing river. By a few simple touches he has given the parable a more general coloring but, from a literary point of view, he has not improved on it. Matthew's version, with its balanced parallelism, its rhythm and its local color, is a faithful rendering of the Aramaic original spoken by our Lord.

However, Luke's variations, readily understandable, have not at all affected the meaning of the parable. The wise man and the foolish man are both disciples, both of them have heard the words of Jesus but only one of them does the words of Christ. At the Last Judgment the doers of the word, and they alone, will stand firm. Probably, the flood-waters may stand as well for any severe trial, and in such a time the price of security will be a life built on active obedience to the teaching of Christ. Both evangelists have explicitly presented the parable as a commentary on the saying: "Not every one who says to me, 'Lord! Lord!' shall enter into the kingdom of Heaven, but only he who does the will of my Father who is in heaven" (Matt. 7, 21; cf. Luke 6, 47).

MASTER AND SERVANT
Luke 17, 7-10

7. But which of you, having a slave plowing or tending sheep, will say to him on his return from the field, "Come at once and sit down to dinner"? 8. Wilt thou not rather say to him, "Get something ready for my dinner; then gird thyself, and wait upon me while I eat and drink, and after this thou shalt eat and drink"? 9. Does he thank that slave for carrying out his orders? 10. I think not. Just so you also, when you have done everything you have been commanded to

do, should say, "We are unprofitable servants! we have but done what it was our
duty to do."

Luke begins chapter 17 with the phrase: "He
also said to his disciples" and this time we can
be sure that the subsequent parable was also addressed to them. It cannot be objected that, so
far as we know, none of the apostles was a farmer
or had kept a slave because the expression "which
of you" (*tis ex humon*) means: "Can you imagine
that . . ."[2] We might render verse 7: "Can you
imagine that any of you would say to his slave
who had come in from plowing or tending sheep,
'Come at once and sit down at table'?"

The situation is altogether hypothetical. The
farmer of the parable is not a wealthy man since
he has only one slave who must do the farm work
and also serve at table. As a slave there is no
question of wages for his service nor does the
master see why he should thank the slave for
carrying out his orders (verse 9). Jesus himself
draws out the moral in verse 10: the disciples,
God's slaves, have no claim to reward for doing
what God expects of them; they must humbly
acknowledge that they are but poor servants. In
the context, "unprofitable" is not the best rendering — "poor," "humble" would be better so there
is no suggestion that man's works are useless (*cf*. Matt 25, 31-46). What does follow is
that the reward of virtue, of good works, is a
free gift of God, and men have no right to it.
This teaching is in contrast to the view of the
Pharisees, and the disciples would have recognized that.

THE WAITING SERVANTS
Luke 12, 35-38; (Mark 13, 33-37)

35. Let your loins be girded and your lamps burning, 36. and you yourselves like men waiting for their master when he returns from the wedding; so that when he comes and knocks they may at once open to him. 37. Happy are those servants whom their master, when he comes, shall find watching. Indeed I tell you that he will gird himself, and make them recline at table, and go about and serve them. 38. And if he comes in the second watch, or if he comes in the third watch, and finds them thus, happy are those servants.

33. Take heed, watch and pray, for you do not know when the time is: 34. it is as when a man, traveling abroad, on leaving his house gave authority to his servants—to each one his own task — and commanded the porter to watch. 35. Watch, therefore — for you know not when the master of the house will come, whether in the evening, or at midnight, or at cockcrow, or in the morning—36. lest coming suddenly he find you sleeping. 37. But what I say to you I say to all—Watch!

The two versions of this parable, in Luke and Mark, differ rather widely in detail. Both evangelists have understood it in terms of the Parousia but it can easily be seen how allegorical additions in Luke's form have heightened the application. The short verse 35 is probably Luke's intro-

duction to the series of parables (verses 36-48),
an exhortation to constant vigilance (the skirts
of the long outer garment were tucked into the
cincture for freedom of movement; the lamps
must be ready and lighted—the ancient oil lamp
cannot be lit by pressing a switch!), and *The
Waiting Servants* really begins at verse 36. The
servants are expected to sit up for their master
who is returning from a wedding—in Mark he
has been on a journey. If we exclude verse 37b
the parable follows in much the same way in
Mark. True, Mark (verse 35) follows the Roman
fourfold division of the night and Luke (verse
37) gives the three Jewish watches, but this is
hardly significant. More important is the fact
that Mark insists on watchfulness while Luke
stresses the reward of vigilance.

However, in verse 37b, Luke has an addition
which points to the identity of the master because,
unlike any earthly master, he himself will serve
the faithful servants (*cf.* 17, 7-8). Two texts
spring to mind: "I am in the midst of you as he
that serves" (22, 27) and "I, the Lord and the
Master, have washed your feet" (John 13, 14).
This "Master" is evidently the Lord who welcomes his faithful servants to the Messianic Feast
and through this allegorical detail the message
of the parable has been underlined. From verse
22 of the chapter onward Jesus had been speaking to his disciples (*cf.* verse 32); it is to them
that *The Waiting Servants* is addressed, one of
his frequent warnings to wakefulness and vigilance. The coming of the Son of Man will be
unexpected and watchfulness must characterize

the attitude of the disciple who waits for his return.

THE THIEF AT NIGHT
Luke 12, 39-40 (Cf. Matt. 34, 43-44)

39. But be sure of this, that if the householder had known at what hour the thief was coming, he would have watched, and not have suffered his house to be broken into. 40. Be you also ready; for at an unexpected moment the Son of Man will come.

This little parable points to the uncertainty of the hour at which the Lord will return, for, indeed, the Lord will come "like a thief in the night" (1 Thess. 5, 2). The householder is not in the same situation as the servants of the previous parable. They knew the night of their master's return—though not the precise hour—and so they could keep watch; the householder has no idea when his house is going to be burglarized. Therefore the moral, expressed in verse 40, is not vigilance as before but preparedness: the Son of Man will appear as Judge at an unexpected moment. It is by association of ideas that the parable has been inserted here—the reference to watching in verse 39 and mention of the coming of the Son of Man in verse 40.

THE FRIEND AT MIDNIGHT
Luke 11, 5-8

5. Suppose one of you has a friend, to whom he goes at midnight and says, "Friend, lend

me three loaves; 6. for a friend of mine has arrived at my house from a journey, and I have nothing to set before him"; 7. and he, answering from within, says, "Don't bother me; the door is now fastened, and my children and I are in bed; I cannot get up and give them to you." 8. I tell you, though he will not get up and give them to him because he is his friend, yet because his friend persists, he will rise and give him as many as he needs.

In the passage 11, 1-13 Luke gives us a synthesis of our Lord's teaching on prayer—beginning with the Our Father. In this context the parable usually known as *The Importunate Friend* certainly has to do with perseverance in prayer. But we may ask whether it had this meaning originally.

Before discussing the point it would be well to explain certain details of the typically Palestinian setting. We must imagine a small village, without shops. Bread was baked in the very early morning so the man who lent the loaves was not seriously inconvenienced—fresh bread would be available for breakfast. Three of the flat, round loaves (verse 5) was reckoned to be a meal for one man; the reception of the guest has to be measured by the oriental code of hospitality. The village house would have consisted of a single room and the "bed" was a mat on which the whole family slept; the opening of the door would involve disturbing the children stretched on the floor.

As suggested above, we should abstract from

the present context if we are to understand the original purpose of the parable. Then it becomes clear that, as Jesus spoke it, it had not to do with persevering prayer; the emphasis was not on the action of the one who had come to ask but on the attitude of the other. We have explained earlier[3] that the phrase *tis ex humon* introduces a rhetorical question, a question which runs on to the end of verse 7. A refusal of the request is regarded as unthinkable—a blatant breach of the code of hospitality, it would cast an unforgivable slur on the whole village.

Yet, for the sake of argument, our Lord supposes that if the man is to be moved neither by friendship nor by convention he will at least grant the request in order to be rid of the other. All the while it is the man within who is in question and the point is that he is going to grant the request without fail. The teaching does concern prayer and its implication is evident: if this man acts so, how much more will God hearken to those who call upon him. He cannot fail to hear them. Our Lord insists that prayer must be *trustful;* his disciples must have unshaken confidence in the goodness of their Father. And if St. Luke has found in the parable a lesson on perseverance in prayer, is not perseverance the consequence of trust?

THE UNJUST JUDGE
Luke 18, 1-8

1. He also told them a parable to the effect that they ought to pray at all times and not grow faint-hearted.
2. "There was a judge," said he, "in a certain town, who neither feared God, nor had regard for man. 3. And there was a widow in that town who kept coming to him, saying, 'Give me judgment against my adversary.' 4. He would not, however, for a while; but afterward he said to himself, 'Although I neither fear God nor have any regard for man, 5. yet, because this widow is troublesome to me, I will give judgment in her favor, or she will have me worn out with her incessant visits.' "
6. "Hear, now," the Lord added, "what this unjust judge says. 7. And will not God avenge his elect, who cry to him day and night, and will he delay long over their case? 8. I tell you, he will avenge them speedily. However, when the Son of Man comes, will he find faith on the earth?"

This time Luke leaves us in no doubt at all about his application of the parable: the disciples should pray at all times and persevere in it (*cf.* 1 Thess. 5, 17). In reality, as we shall see, the parable is closely parallel to *The Friend at Midnight* and originally would have had the same purport.

The judge, described as unjust in verse 6, is of a type that was all too common in Israel (*cf.* Amos 5, 7, 10-13; Isa. 1, 23; 5, 7-23; Jer. 5, 28).

And the Old Testament also often refers to the helpless widow (Ex. 22, 21f; Deut. 10, 18; Isa. 1, 17; Jer. 22, 3). It is evident that the widow of the parable has right on her side, but the judge is not interested in the right or wrong of a penniless plaintiff; if he is to give a decision in favor of anybody it has to be made worthwhile for him. However, this time he has met his match because the woman is not going to be put off and continues to pester him. Finally the judge admits it cynically to himself. He hears her and gives judgment in her favor only because she had made such a nuisance of herself that he wanted to be rid of her.

Our Lord draws special attention to the words of the judge, so it is plain that, as he spoke the parable, the emphasis lay on the judge and not on the widow's entreaties. The lesson that Jesus teaches here is confidence in prayer; it is not a question, then, of how we ought to pray but rather of God's attention to our prayers. If so callous a man as the unjust judge is moved — if only from a purely selfish motive—by the entreaties of a helpless widow, how much more will God, the merciful Father, hear the cries of his elect. Indeed he will speedily help them.

The last sentence (verse 8b) can scarcely have been part of the original parable. It has no contact with the story of the widow and the judge, the Son of Man appears too abruptly; it is surely an isolated saying of Jesus added here by Luke. In its present context, spoken to the disciples (verse 1), its meaning appears to be: they, the elect, have nothing to fear, they will be heard by God; but will the Son of Man, at his second coming, find men like them, will he find faith on the earth? The saying is an echo of Matt. 24, 12—"On account of the increasing lawlessness, the love of the majority will be chilled."

Although, like *The Friend at Midnight*, this parable, also, originally referred to the certainty of God's attention to the prayers of his elect, it is even more readily understandable that, in view of the widow's determination to keep on pestering the judge, it should have been taken by the early Christians as an admonition to perseverance in prayer.

THE GOOD SAMARITAN
Luke 10, 30-37

25. And a doctor of the Law rose to test him, and asked, "Master, what must I do in order to inherit eternal life?" 26. "What is written in the Law," he asked him; "how dost thou read it?" 27. He answered, *"Thou shalt love the Lord thy God with thy whole heart, and with thy whole soul, and with thy whole strength, and with thy whole mind";* and *"thy neighbor as thyself."* 28. "Thou hast answered rightly," he replied; "do that, and thou shalt live." 29. Wishing, however, to justify himself, he asked Jesus, "And who is my neighbor?"

30. Jesus taking him up said: "A man, on his way down from Jerusalem to Jericho, fell among robbers, who both stripped and beat him, and then departed leaving him half dead. 31. Now by chance a certain

priest was going down that road, who, at
sight of him, passed by on the other side.
32. Likewise, a Levite also, when he came
to the place and saw him, passed by on the
other side. 33. But a certain Samaritan who
was traveling came to where he was, and on
seeing him took pity on him. 34. and went to
him and bandaged his wounds, pouring on
oil and wine. Then seating him on his own
beast he conveyed him to an inn, and took
care of him. 35. And the next day, taking
out two denarii, he gave them to the landlord, and said, 'Take care of him; and whatever thou dost spend besides I will pay thee
on my return.' 36. Which of these three,
dost thou think, proved neighbor to him who
fell among the robbers" 37. "He who performed the work of mercy on him," was the
reply. "Go," said Jesus to him, "and do the
like thyself."

The introductory passage (10, 25-29) is essential for an understanding of *The Good Samaritan* because the parable is a reply to the questions
of the scribe. His first question: "What must I do
in order to inherit eternal life?" was intended to
embarrass Jesus, but our Lord, adroitly, put the
onus on the questioner. So the lawyer tried again
and asked for a definition of "neighbor." This
time he must have felt that the "Master" would
have difficulty in answering for it was, in fact,
a much discussed question. The Pharisees would
have excluded all non-Pharisees while the Es-
senes of Qumran would go even further and
declare that all the "sons of darkness" *i.e.,* all
who did not belong to the sect, should be hated.

All would agree that, even in the broadest interpretation, the term should be limited to Jews and proselytes. It is expected that Jesus, too, will respect these limits; it remains to be seen whether he would narrow them appreciably.

The story that Jesus proceeds to tell illustrates at once the working of the Semitic mind and the purpose of a parable. A question has been asked which, to one of Greek culture, begs for a clear-cut definition. The approach of Jesus is very different but his method is perfectly acceptable to the lawyer who unerringly grasps the point of the parable (verse 37).

Though the story does not concern an historical incident its setting is very credible. The road from Jerusalem to Jericho was, until recent times, a dangerous one for lone travelers. The brigands were members of local Bedouin tribes who knew the wild country inside out and were practically immune from effective pursuit. But in this all too familiar background the parable Jesus relates is highly distinctive.

Though it is not explicitly stated it is certainly implied that the man who was waylaid on the road was a Jew. His nationality is not expressly mentioned because the very point of the parable is that the lawyer's problem is not going to be solved in terms of nationality or race. The priest chanced to be going along the same road and carefully avoided the wounded man. A suggestion that he supposed him to be dead and did not wish to incur ritual impurity by contact with a corpse is foreign to the perspective of the parable; besides, he was coming from Jerusalem — his period of Temple service was over. We are to surmise quite simply that he did not want to get involved in what, one way or another, was sure to be a messy business. The Levite took the same selfish course. Jesus does not accuse them of callousness, he does not pass judgment on their conduct. They are men who lack the courage to love—dare we say that they represent the average man?

After the priest and Levite it might have been expected that the third traveler—a series of three is typical of the popular story—would turn out to be a Jewish layman; the bias would be in some way anti-clerical. The drama is that the third man, and the hero of the story, is one of the hated Samaritans. He has been designedly chosen to bring out the essential unselfishness of love.

This man applied first aid to the wounded traveler and, curiously, in verse 34, Luke has put the ministrations in inverse order for the wounds would have been first washed with wine—regarded as a disinfectant— then dressed with oil and bandaged. His beast was almost certainly a donkey so the Samaritan would have had to walk beside the animal, supporting the injured man. And when he came to the inn he did not feel that his obligations had ended. Whatever a cynic might have thought of his conduct so far, the man turns out to be a realist. He did not naively presume on the charity of the innkeeper but paid him two denarii (a denarius represented a day's wages) and assured him that he would settle any further accounts when he returned that way. Apparently the Samaritan was a merchant—on a very modest scale no doubt—who plied between his own country and Jerusalem.

At the end, Jesus got the lawyer to answer his own question. Yet, did he really answer the original question? In verse 29 he asked: "Who is my neighbor?" while the question that Jesus put to him in verse 36 is rather: "To whom am I neighbor?"—the very question indicates the difference there is between the Jewish outlook and Christian charity. The lawyer was concerned with the object of love and his question implied a limitation: my neighbor is one who belongs to such and such a group. Jesus was interested in the subject of love: which of the three had acted as neighbor? The lawyer's question was not answered because it was a mistaken question. A man cannot determine theoretically who his neighbor is simply because love is not theory but practice.

A man's neighbor is any man who needs his help, says the parable; the wounded man was neighbor to the priest and Levite just as much as he was to the Samaritan, but while they theorized in the manner of the lawyer, he acted. The traveler was neighbor to all three; the Samaritan alone was neighbor in return. The lawyer had learned his lesson and answered correctly. A frequent suggestion that he deliberately avoided pronouncing the hated name "Samaritan" is doubtless unfair to him; in fact his answer does underline the message of the Savior — "he who performed the work of mercy on him."

Though the final recommendation of Christ was addressed to the lawyer it contains a message, and a warning, for all Christians. We must not pause to ask ourselves: "Is this man really my neighbor?" for a question like this has no place in the Christian life. Christian charity knows no bounds and oversteps all man-made limits. The pity is that there are so few Samaritans among us.

List of Parables

LUKE

MATTHEW

MARK

Footnotes

Chapter I

1. Joachim Jeremias, *Die Gleichnisse Jesu,* Göttingen 1956, p. 5.
2. C. H. Dodd, *The Parables of the Kingdom,* London 1936, p. 16.
3. C. H. Dodd, *op. cit.,* p. 18.
4. The text also occurs in the parallel passages: Matt. 13, 10-15 and Luke 8, 9-10—but the other evangelists have followed Mark.
5. C. H. Dodd, *op. cit.,* p. 15.
6. J. Jeremias, *op. cit.,* pp. 7-12.
7. The same text of Isaiah occurs in the following passages: Matt. 13, 14-15; Luke 8, 10 and also in John 12, 40. In Acts 28, 25-27 St. Paul applies it to the Jewish reaction to his preaching.
8. The passive "has been given" (*cf.* also verse 12 "be forgiven") is a circumlocution for "God". The Jews sought to avoid mention of the name of God whenever possible and in speaking to them, Jesus followed the convention.

Chapter II

1. A. M. Hunter, *Introducing the Parables,* London 1960, pp. 25-26.
2. *Quaestiones Evangeliorum* II, 19. *Cf.* C. H. Dodd, *op. cit.,* pp. 11-12.
3. F. A. Reuter, *Homiletic Sermonettes on the Gospels,* St. Louis 1925, pp. 263f.
4. Further examples of such fusion of parables are, among others, Matt. 12, 33-37; Luke 6, 43-45; 13, 24-30.
5. A. George, "Parabole", *Dictionnaire de la Bible* (Supplément), VI, Paris, 1960, c. 1161.

Chapter III

1. J. Jeremias, *op. cit.,* p. 119.
2. "Heaven" is a typical Jewish substitution for "God". *Cf.* Matthew's "kingdom of heaven" for

"kingdom of God". J. Jeremias, *op. cit.*, pp. 117-118 renders the verse: "Thus will God rejoice more over one sinner who has repented than over ninety-nine respectable persons who have never committed any grave sin."

3. *Ibid.* p. 28.
4. *Ibid.* p. 29.
5. C. H. Dodd, *op. cit.*, p. 151.

CHAPTER IV

1. *Cf.* Matt. 6, 27; 7, 9; 12, 11; Luke 11, 11; 12, 25; 14, 5. 28; 15, 4; 17, 7 etc.
2. J. Jeremias, *op. cit.*, p. 138.
3. In Palestinian weddings the round dance was danced by men; the funeral lament was the women's concern. J. Jeremias, *op. cit.*, pp. 139f.
4. C. H. Dodd, *op. cit.*, pp. 28-29.
5. See pp. 46-48.
6. A. M. Hunter, *op. cit.*, p. 88.
7. J. Jeremias, *op. cit.*, p. 127.
8. A. George, *art. cit.*, c. 1173.

CHAPTER V

1. See p. 16f.
2. "Eschatological" comes from the Greek *eschata* = the last things. Eschatology is teaching concerning the last things—the close of this present age and the end of the world. In a real sense, of course, with the coming of Christ the last age has begun; but there remains the consummation.
3. Pp. 20-23.
4. See p. 18.
5. J. Jeremias, *op. cit.*, p. 130.
6. My translation. See p. 56.

CHAPTER VI

1. A. M. Hunter, *op. cit.*, p. 84.
2. In rabbinical law, the man who had buried a deposit immediately he had received it was free from blame; but one who had merely wrapped it in a cloth would be held responsible for its loss. J. Jeremias, *op. cit.*, p. 53.

3. P. 49f.
4. My translation.
5. Throughout Luke *ho kyrios* almost always means our Lord. Besides, verse 8b is out of place in the mouth of the steward's master — who, moreover, would scarcely have praised his deceitful servant.
6. J. Jeremias, *op. cit.,* p. 35. From rabbinical writings we learn that good works were termed "friends", "spokesmen"—they spoke in favor of one. Hence, "make to yourselves friends" means, "Do good works". The phrase, "they may receive" would seem to cloak the divine name: "God may receive you".
7. Parallelism is a figure of speech distinctive of Semitic poetry; it is prominent in the Old Testament and often occurs in sayings of our Lord. In synonymous parallelism the two members of a couplet express the same idea: the second renders the sense of the first in different words.
8. A. George, *art. cit.,* c. 1161.

Chapter VII

1. Pp. 28-35.
2. b. Ber 28b. Strack-Billerbeck, *Kommentar zum Neuen Testament aus Talmud und Midrasch* II, München 1924, p. 240. *Cf.* J. Jeremias, *op. cit.,* p. 124.
3. Verse 14 should be rendered: "This man went back to his house justified, the other not."
4. "Sinners" means people who led an immoral life (*e.g.,* adulterers, unjust—Luke 18, 11) and those who followed a way of life which involved dishonesty or immorality (*e.g.,* tax-collectors and even shepherds). All such had lost their civil rights and their work was regarded as incompatible with observance of the Law. See J. Jeremias, *op. cit.,* p. 116.
5. *The New English Bible* (New Testament), Oxford/Cambridge 1961.

Chapter VIII

1. A. M. Hunter, *op. cit.,* p. 65.
2. See p. 57.
3. See pp. 57, 141.

Select Bibliography

DODD, C. H. *The Parables of the Kingdom* (3rd ed.), London, 1936.

GEORGE, A. "Parabole," *Dictionnaire de la Bible* (Supplement) VI, Paris, 1960. cc. 1149-1177.

HUNTER, A. M. *Interpreting the Parables*, London, 1960.

JEREMIAS, JOACHIM. *Die Gleichnisse Jesu* (4th ed.), Gottingen, 1956.

LAGRANGE, M.-J. *Evangile selon Saint Luc*, Paris, 1921.

OSTY, E. *L'Evangile selon Saint Luc* (BJ) (3rd ed.), Paris, 1961.

SCHMID, J. *Das Evangelium nach Lukas* (4th ed.), Regensburg, 1960.